WHERE IS THE EVIDENCE?

FINDING THE TRUTH IN THE GOSPEL OF JOHN

WHERE IS THE EVIDENCE?

FINDING THE TRUTH IN THE GOSPEL OF JOHN

ALEXANDER WOOLLEY

Matador
Unit E2 Airfield Business Park,
Harrison Road, Market Harborough,
Leicestershire. LE16 7UL
Tel: 0116 2792299
Email: books@troubador.co.uk
Web: www.troubador.co.uk/matador
Twitter: @matadorbooks

ISBN 978 1803131 108

British Library Cataloguing in Publication Data.
A catalogue record for this book is available from the British Library.

Printed and bound by CPI Group (UK) Ltd, Croydon, CR0 4YY
Typeset in 12pt Adobe Caslon Pro by Troubador Publishing Ltd, Leicester, UK

Matador is an imprint of Troubador Publishing Ltd

Dedicated to Balliol College, Oxford, where I learned about methods of thinking and evaluation of evidence, and to Margaret, my wife, whose devotion has kept me alive long enough to produce this book.

CONTENTS

—

PROLOGUE

A hundred and fifty years ago, the idea that there had actually been a Trojan war was regarded by many as a fairy tale, not very different from thinking that there was a god called Vulcan who lived inside the volcano, Mount Etna. However, archaeological work in the area of the supposed site of Troy in modern Turkey and more careful analysis of the dating of the language in Homer's Iliad, as well as other historical research, have demonstrated that the idea that there was a war between the Greeks and the people who lived where the 'mythical' Troy was found, may well be right. For instance, the Trojan Horse may have had foundation in fact: Hittite horsemen, supposed allies of the Trojans, may have switched sides and helped the Greeks to enter Troy. Heinrich Schliemann and subsequent scholars have taught people to think differently. Similarly, in Science, re-evaluation of old evidence may produce new theories and ways of seeing matters. In just the same way, as what Jesus taught is important, it would help if we realised that a re-assessment of the stories about what Jesus did while he preached could be very valuable. We might then be able to trust the message better and appreciate more fully the authority of its source.

John Ashton, one of the most formidable scholars to study the Gospel according to John, was sure that the accounts of the resurrection of Jesus, as well as of the other 'miracles', were without any historical significance, just like the stories of Santa Claus delivering presents at Christmas. It may be argued that Ashton, along with others who are self-declared atheists, such as Richard Dawkins, are in the same position as were those who believed there was no factual basis for the Trojan War. A fresh look and a new way of conducting a review of the evidence that is actually available will, it is argued, produce very profitable results.

ONE

—

INTRODUCTION TO COMPARING THE VALUE OF THE FOUR GOSPELS' VERSIONS OF THE LIFE OF JESUS AND WHAT HE TAUGHT

I f God does not exist, it probably does not matter very much if we are theist, deist, agnostic or even atheist, although this latter belief cannot logically be held by a finite mind, because the possibilities are, at least theoretically, infinite; on the other hand, if God does exist, it is clear that what we believe may be a little more important. Secondly, if faith matters, it is helpful if that faith has solid foundations, based on evidence that can be sufficiently reliably established so as to be acceptable as historical truth. We might bear in mind that, when the writer of the Gospel according to John wrote of truth, he meant, also, divine reality.

Is there any trustworthy evidence to help us decide what we may believe to be real in material terms and with a faith that is firm? I believe there is, and in this short book we are trying not only to find that evidence but also to establish the quality of that evidence, by evaluating the validity of its sources. An important consideration may be how to deal with conflicting evidence; if we can see that a particular piece of evidence has better provenance than another piece of evidence, when the two appear to conflict, we do not need, artificially, to try to reconcile the different accounts: we can simply decide which is the better, the more likely account, by using the *best sourced evidence*. Occasionally, the conflict between two or more pieces of evidence about a particular event might appear to weaken the credibility of it all, until we manage to assess the evidence exhaustively.

Some years ago, Margaret, my wife, and I were spending the day with the Sisters of Bethany, in Southsea, Portsmouth, when something induced me to suggest to a nun that Christianity was like a Christmas tree, hidden by its decorations. The nun seemed to agree. If we want to see what is true and credible, we should try looking for that truth after removing the decorations, as they may distract us with their beguiling camouflage, when we are trying to assess the value of that evidence.

Mark's Gospel did not give any information about Jesus's life before he was baptised by John, while Matthew and Luke felt that the gap should be filled. It is true that Mark may have felt that the claims that Jesus was descended from David needed a cautionary check. He wrote this about the Messiahship and parentage of Jesus (12:35-40): 'While he was teaching in the temple courts he asked, "Why do the teachers of the law say that the Messiah is the son of David? David himself, speaking by the Holy Spirit declared 'The Lord said to my Lord: "Sit at my right hand until I put your enemies under your feet."'

' "David himself calls him Lord. How then can he be his son?"' Mark is implying that Jesus is too important to be called a son of David.

The writers of Matthew and Luke will have tried to find out something from people who could have known about Jesus's life before his ministry, but when they discovered almost nothing that was satisfactory, they tried to work out for themselves what must have happened by using prophecies in the Old Testament, while ensuring it was appropriate for the one who had been God's only direct representative ever to appear on earth. It is clear that they had obtained no well-attested information, because their two infancy and childhood accounts agreed on nothing except that Jesus was born in Bethlehem and to a virgin mother, which he probably was not; the idea of the mother of Jesus being a virgin was based on an earlier mistranslation of a word that meant a young woman. In placing the birthplace in Bethlehem, Luke imagined Jesus was born in the stable of an inn, while Matthew decided that his parents already lived in a house in Bethlehem, so he said Jesus was born in that. Even their genealogies do not tally; at least that of Matthew starts only with Abraham, who may well be historical, but that of Luke, starting with Jesus, giving his 'supposed' father as Joseph, goes back, quite implausibly, to Adam. It is most unwise to claim that this must be incontrovertible fact on the grounds that every word in the Bible is the inspired and unalterable word of God: the only human to utter words that we may deduce to have come directly from God was Jesus, and even these words we have to calculate from fallible, usually translated and sometimes mistranslated, albeit well-intentioned, accounts in human records. Errors also crept in when the texts were being dictated to copyists, and later scholars tried to emend some of these errors, although they then sometimes compounded the mistakes.

An example of a decoration might be the idea that Jesus came to be born in the stable of an otherwise fully-booked inn, as Luke calculated, on the grounds that there was a census when he was said to have been born, and that the authorities required the family to be there for the census. The writers of Luke and Matthew, as well as of Mark, and to a lesser extent John, were convinced that Jesus was the Jewish Messiah foretold by the prophets, Christ in the Greek form. According to general tradition the Messiah, a future saviour king of Israel, was to be a descendant of King David and born in Bethlehem, although there is one indication in John that no one would know where the Messiah was to come from (7:27). However, John seems to confirm the general tradition in v. 42 and also at the end of the chapter, where the authorities declare, without any contrary indication from the writer, that the Messiah was not to come from Galilee, where Jesus had been born. Luke wanted to have Jesus born in Bethlehem to fit in with the prophecy, so he carefully worked out reasons for Jesus's mother to be there for the birth of Jesus. Unfortunately for his arguments, Nazareth was in a different jurisdiction from that of Bethlehem, so there seems to have been no requirement, at that time, for people from Nazareth to go to Bethlehem for any census, supposing there was one when Jesus was born. Interestingly, Luke seems to acknowledge that Jesus lived in a different jurisdiction at the time of the crucifixion when he says that Jesus, being from Galilee, was in Herod's (Antipas) tetrarchy. There was a census in 6 AD, but that was rather later than Jesus was thought to have been born. According to Matthew, who says quite clearly that it was *Joseph* who was the descendant of David, the family had to leave Bethlehem to escape Herod's otherwise unrecorded massacre of male children who were two years old and under. Matthew was following what Hosea had written, 'When *Israel* was a child, I loved him, and *out of Egypt I called my son* [Israel, not Jesus]' but Hosea had gone on to say 'The more I called them [not *one* son], the more they went from me; they kept sacrificing to the Baals and burning incense to idols', which neither Jesus nor his parents could be accused of doing. Matthew has shown that he may not have got everything right. He went on to support the theory of the massacre by quoting Jeremiah (31:15), saying that the long dead favourite wife of Jacob, Rachel (not Mary), was weeping for her children in Ramah (which is not Bethlehem), and Jeremiah had then gone on to say that there was no need to worry, as the children would come back from the land of the enemy, which might be difficult if they had all been massacred. Interestingly, seeking refuge in the land of the *enemy*, which Joseph and Mary were said to have done to save their son, would not seem such a wise idea, although it would appear that Egypt was considered a good place for refuge as there were Jews living there. Matthew may have made more mistakes. Apparently, Herod the Great did murder a wife, her mother and three of his sons, which might have given rise to the otherwise unsubstantiated idea of a massacre. Lending credence to this grisly reputation, Augustus, the first

Roman Emperor, is reputed to have said he would rather be Herod's pig than Herod's son. Incidentally, if the parents of Jesus were actually poor, would they have been able to pay much tax?

A much less credible decoration is the idea that there were shepherds sitting around in fields at night. Shepherds kept their sheep in enclosed folds at night. Also, as grass for feeding sheep was relatively scarce, it is very unlikely that a significant number of shepherds with their flocks would have all been in the same area at the same moment, even if the flocks were limited to the possibly traditional 100 (Matthew 18:12). Shepherds, like the rest of us, need to sleep at some time, anyway, and what they could see at night would not have been very useful when it came to providing proper protection for their flocks. During the day, however, when they could see properly, they were more brilliant with slings and stones than Robin Hood would be later with bow and arrows or William Tell with a crossbow. They could discourage a sheep from straying by slinging a stone so that it would land just in front of it. David, a very young shepherd, had been remarkably accurate with a sling when he struck Goliath's forehead with penetrating power. Wolves would have been easier targets during daylight. When what seems nonsense to some people is paraded as if it is divinely-inspired truth, which one has fully and firmly to believe if one is to be accepted as a true Christian, there is foolishness on a grand scale.

Even though the ideas be beautiful and the language mesmerising, these fancies may do great damage to the general acceptability, as well as to the credibility, of the message.

It is true that individual instances in the Gospels of unusual wording seem to prove that an actual saying of Jesus is almost certainly being reported. We have such an example when Luke, in chapter 11 vv. 39-41, quotes Jesus as saying in verse 41, "Give alms for those things that are within; and behold everything is clean to you", just after he has said in vv. 39 and 40, "Now you Pharisees cleanse the outside of the cup and of the dish, but inside you are full of extortion and wickedness. You fools! Did not he who made the outside make the inside also?" The word 'alms' has nothing directly to do with cleanliness in this context. However, the Aramaic words for alms (zakkau) and cleanse (dakkau) are very similar and were probably confused in this instance, thus demonstrating that there is very likely to be an authentic basis for this saying: Luke's mistaken grasp of the language shows that he was using something he did not properly understand, so he is unlikely to have invented it: we may deduce that this is based on something that can be attributed to Jesus. Another example is to be found when Mark's version (Mark 10:17 & 18) of the first part of Jesus's answer to a question put to him is "Why do you call me good? No one is good but God alone," whereas Matthew (19:17) has "Why do you *ask* me *about* what is good?". Mark's version, which suggests that Jesus is *not* God, is changed by Matthew so that Jesus may be thought of as God after all. The authenticity of the saying is indicated by this disagreement, while the original and genuine version is more likely to be the one found in Mark, rather than the one in Matthew. One may remember that John, too, implies that Jesus is not God, when he has Jesus saying "God is greater than I am" (14:28).

On the other hand, there is extensive evidence available which is very good indeed. C.S. Lewis, when reviewing the stories in the Gospel according to John, noted that the stories there could not have been invented when the Gospel was written, as the literary skills and artifice required for such a style of invention did not exist at that time and did not come into existence till very many centuries later. Furthermore, the detailed knowledge of Palestine, as it had been in Jesus's lifetime, and the details recounted in events such as the trial scenes of Jesus, demonstrate such precise and detailed knowledge that only an eyewitness of the actual events would have been able to provide it: such detailed knowledge of the background had been lost well before the last Gospel came to be written down. As a result, we are in a position to believe that the important components of the stories in John's Gospel are a witness's faithful recollections of what actually happened. The theology in John, however, has almost certainly *not* been garnered from the witness and would appear to have been composed as imaginatively as the stories in Luke. Nonetheless, both the theology in John and Luke's stories, particularly his 'canticles', are wonderful, and together these two writers are very useful, if not essential, in helping us to appreciate the vital aura of Jesus's teaching and ministry.

One should note that a disciple called John figures prominently in the other Gospels and in Acts of the Apostles, often as as a companion of Peter, but he is not mentioned by that name in John's Gospel. He must have been in the Gospel, but is not specifically identified. He will have been, therefore, one may naturally deduce, sometimes 'The Disciple whom Jesus loved' (a title probably conferred by the writer of the Gospel and used in 13:23-25; 19:25-27; 20:2; 21:20, 'a disciple' (one of the two who were the first to follow Jesus), or 'another disciple' or 'that disciple'. In the last chapter, again unidentified, he was probably one of the 'two other disciples' who were, actually, the two sons of Zebedee; it is suggested that there was *not* an extra pair, who went on the fishing expedition. The other of the two disciples was probably John's brother, James. Five, the number of the first group of disciples that attended the wedding in Cana rather than seven, in a Galilee fishing boat, might seem quite enough. John is not identified by name because actually to name a person was to endanger that person when still alive: Christians, as they had come to be known by the time this last Gospel was written, were frequent targets for persecution or worse. We have different titles for this anonymous disciple, who may be deduced to have been very important because of the significance of the occasions on which he is mentioned. The double source of the Gospel suggests that the description, 'The disciple whom Jesus loved', was assigned by the writer when he was giving *his* version of events, and the other descriptions were assigned to the disciple when the writer was following more closely the information he was receiving from this witnessing disciple.

To disentangle reliable evidence from the rest of John's Gospel is not always seriously challenging, but it may help to know what is what if we can work out how the Gospel came to be written down in the first place. With the first three Gospels the explanation is probably along the following lines. Nothing was written down to begin with, as Jesus was expected to return very soon indeed. People might have confused his quick return after the crucifixion with the idea of another quick return. He did not, however, return again. It is possible that Peter had been crucified before anyone realised the extent to which those who still had personal memories of what had actually happened were being reduced in number by death. Material, which was now being lost so regularly, was needed for the account.

It is recorded that a man called John Mark, a

companion of Paul, had accompanied Peter as a helper (interpreter or personal assistant, whose job was to explain what Peter actually meant) when he was spreading the message of Jesus. This man, according to accounts, was used by Peter, as he could not only, one imagines, read and write, but also understood Greek, the lingua franca, far better than the illiterate Peter, whose mother tongue was Aramaic. He seems to have written notes to help to explain to other people what Peter had been talking about, when such explanations were required. These notes will have been handed on at sometime, without any chronological indication as to when the different events had happened, and then used to produce the first Gospel according to Mark. One might note, in passing, that the Gospel according to John, whose chronology may be trusted better, gives three Passover festivals as opposed to just one in the other Gospels, implying that the ministry lasted more than two years.

Mark's Gospel might have appeared in about 67 AD. When this happened, other people will have remembered other things that had not been mentioned in the newly produced Gospel. Some of these things, especially sayings, will have been written down by people and then used later to develop the Gospels according to Matthew and Luke. The first three Gospels were based on second- or third-hand information, the two later versions, named Matthew and Luke, being based very extensively on the first one attributed to Mark, while they incorporated some of the new material, each writer choosing from this what suited his line of presentation. It is clear that the information provided by Mark was considered superior to that more recently available, as the writers often made differing selections from the new sources and used what they had access to in Mark conjointly far more frequently.

The last Gospel, according to John, would appear to have had a totally different genesis. It is so different from the first three that it seems almost a different story. The writer is clearly an extraordinarily learned Jewish theologian, as well as an arithmetical expert as was demonstrated in his use of numbers (noted particularly by a German scholar, M.J.J. Menken); he knew almost everything that had been written down up to that time, especially the Old Testament. Being based in Ephesus, where the Gospel is said to have been written, he may have met Paul there, that most prominent of all Jesus's missionaries, during Paul's three year stay in Ephesus, and might even have known of some of Paul's letters, as he wrote his first letter to the Corinthians there. John, the writer, may not have written anything himself up till then, as his views were probably both too firmly developed and too different from anyone else's. Nevertheless, he may have felt that the momentum of the early euphoria that had fired the spread of the Gospel message of Jesus in the early days was now rather feeble; he will have thought that some of the theological developments were not quite as they should be; but he needed new and extremely convincing evidence to correct the theology and reignite the ardour of the missionaries. The writer may even have felt the force of what was to be said about the Laodicean church, in Revelation 3:15, where tepid worshippers will be spewed out of the mouth of God because they are neither hot nor cold: they had to be committed full-heartedly to the service of God, not merely engaged in the ritual performance of a liturgy without being emotionally committed and involved. One might note that the writer of this Gospel is as fiercely pro-'Christian' as Paul had once been against those Jews who had chosen to follow Jesus; he may have alienated many Jews and so was reciprocating the disfavour; this could be why he so repeatedly denigrates Jews in the Gospel. Also, he regularly makes it clear that Jesus is for the whole world, so it is unlikely that he wrote the words in Revelation that the few to be saved at the end of time were to come only from the twelve tribes of Israel.

Thus, when, to his amazement, the writer actually came across someone who had been a devoted and unflagging follower of Jesus, he will have questioned him for days on end to find out every detail the witness could remember. During this excited questioning, he will have written it all down, reformulating his own theological understanding in the process, while adding his explanations and also calculating much of what Jesus had said from what he learned from his illiterate informant.

The informant appears to have had a better memory for stories than sayings and preaching. If someone has personal feelings involved, particularly when ego-promotion or ego-defence is concerned, distortion may easily affect memories. Frequent oral repetition may, to some extent, affect memories as well, so that adjustments might be made during repetition, as there are people for whom being interesting is rather more important than getting every fact right. However, our witness here is not of the self-seeking or self-promoting sort. He seems to have been charming, and charm is associated with gentle, entertaining conversation. He is likely to have spent many hours telling many people of his experiences with Jesus and it is most unlikely that any adjustments were needed to make the picture which he was presenting more attractive.

While he was there he will have told many in the High Priest's household of his experiences with Jesus, but he will not have remembered the actual teaching, which will be one of the reasons for their finding his associating with Jesus perfectly acceptable; he was not, as far as they could tell, being corrupted by what he was experiencing. We may feel it likely that the High Priest's household was as free in what they told him as he was free with what he told them. We may, therefore, almost certainly rely on both the accuracy and comprehensiveness of his memories being as good as they appear to be in the Gospel.

In addition to what he managed to deduce from his informant, the writer will have used his knowledge of the Old Testament, and will have been guided by what he knew of the first three Gospels. He might even have known Paul personally, but Paul's theology was probably too different in style from that of the writer to affect importantly what the writer decided to commit to paper.

We do not know how the witness and writer of John's Gospel met for the first time, but there is a useful story in the Syriac History of John. Stories such as these often have factual foundations but the stories have been embellished out of all recognition. It seems that John, the Son of Zebedee, had gone, when he was still very young, in some sort of exile to the then extremely active Mediterranean port, Ephesus, whose site is now in modern Turkey. This might have been even before Herod Agrippa beheaded his brother, James, in 44 AD. Some decades later, when he was much older, for some reason or other, he decided to gain employment as an attendant at public baths there. One day, when he was at the side of the baths, someone sank, apparently lifeless, beneath the surface. He had help in pulling the body out of the water and something induced him to start pumping the chest of the apparently lifeless man; he pumped out the water from his lungs and then carried on pumping until he happened to get his heart and lungs going again. He seemed to have brought a dead man back to life. At the baths that day was John the Elder, who later wrote the three letters attributed to John of that name. He was amazed, and as a result of his cross-examination of the man who had saved the life of the bather, he learned that this illiterate fellow from Galilee had, as a youth, been a devoted follower of Jesus and had actually witnessed an enormous amount of what Jesus had done, even though he did not remember much of what Jesus had taught, apparently not even the parables. As a result of careful questioning he was able to write the Gospel according to John. It may have been written quickly, but probably not in an hour as the Syriac History of John tells us. Perhaps it would be better if the Gospel was thought of as the Gospel according to 'The Two Johns' rather than just John, as two Johns were responsible for its being written rather than only one. There were, appropriately, according to Eusebius and Dionysius the Great, two *famous* tombs in Ephesus, the one of John the Apostle and the other of John the Elder. Eusebius (c. 260-340 AD) was considered the father of Church History and supported the teaching of Arius who claimed that Jesus and the Holy Spirit were subordinate to God, while Dionysius the Great, who died in about 264 AD, is quoted by Eusebius.

It might be pointed out, in support of Arius, that a communicator (the Holy Spirit) is not necessarily the one who initiates what is communicated, while the direct representative is not the one whom he represents, even though, to all intents and purposes, God, Jesus and the Holy Spirit are united in their aims and work inextricably together: to that extent they *are* one. We should note that Jesus makes it clear quite often that God is greater than he, as in Mark 10:17&18. The Holy Spirit is God's communication system and stems from God alone and executes only the purposes of God, but he is not actually God, although we may quite correctly perceive him to be an aspect of God which is absolutely essential for our spiritual existence. The three may be said to be one, but Jesus, God's only direct representative, and the Holy Spirit, God's communicator, are nevertheless, however uniquely bound up in God's purposes, insofar as we can guess what those purposes might be and how they are being achieved, secondary to the one and only true God to whom we gain access *only* through Jesus and the Holy Spirit. One God, with three personas, but God, our Father, is the source of everything else.

This illiterate follower of Jesus seems to have been the youngest and possibly rather spoilt one of the family, which was rich, as it had hired servants according to Mark's Gospel (1:20). It probably had a house in Jerusalem where the youngest son was based when, we may deduce, he was delivering preserved fish to the High Priest's household. When Jesus was staying in Jerusalem he may well have stayed in this house. It is possible that the last supper took place here too. Business with the inordinately wealthy High Priest will probably have been very lucrative, thus explaining at least some of the source of the wealth of the Zebedee fishing business. This may be why the writer did not say anything about the source of Zebedee's wealth, not even mentioning that he was wealthy. However, Jesus knew he was sufficiently wealthy to look after his mother when, on the cross, he committed her to the home and family of his youngest and most devoted follower, the witness. If the designated mother, the wife of Zebedee, was the sister of Jesus's mother, Mary, this would all make very good sense indeed. It is said her name was Salome.

We learn about the life-style of the youth, early on in the Gospel. He had enough spare time to be following John the Baptist, but remarks made by the Baptist persuaded him and Andrew, Simon Peter's brother, who may have been in a position similar to that of John, that they would be better off following Jesus. They then spent the rest of the day with Jesus. Neither of the two seems to have had a job that needed him to be at it all the time. Andrew, similarly to John, might have had business supplying some rich people in Jerusalem with preserved fish from his brother Peter's fishing business. Judging from the extent of the material which John the witness remembered about Jesus, particularly when one bears in mind how much he says he had left out of his witness at the end of chapter 21, one recognises at once that he must have spent an enormous amount of his time with Jesus, while Jesus's energy and stamina must have been prodigious.

There are chapters that demonstrate that there were times when particular points which were being made by the witness have not been properly understood by the writer, such as when, in chapter 11, the witness has made it clear that Jesus said that Lazarus was asleep – in a coma – while the writer emphasises that Lazarus is dead, because that was what the writer firmly believed. Again, when Jesus washes his disciples' feet in chapter 13, near the beginning of the chapter, the point that Jesus is making is that the servant is as important as his master; indeed, he is showing that the master should also serve his servants. The writer, on the other hand, is keen to explain that the servant, the disciple, is not as great as his master, because he felt that Jesus was a corporeal manifestation of God rather than just human, and no human could be considered the equal of God. It is, nevertheless, clear, that to the witness Jesus was completely human, even if he is the most special human ever to have lived; this was true, as Jesus was being directed by God in a way that no one has been directed before or since. Even more important is the account of where Jesus went after his arrest, in chapter 18.

According to the account in the Gospel, it would appear that the interrogation of Jesus occurred in the house of Annas and that all the action took place there. After this, Jesus was taken to the house of Caiaphas, where nothing is recorded as having happened. However, it is an officer of the High Priest who strikes Jesus. It is into the house of the High Priest that the witnessing disciple arranges for Peter to be admitted. It is in the the High Priest's house that Peter denies knowing Jesus three times.

It is clear that the writer has asked first where they went, on the night of the arrest, and that the witness said that they went first to the house of Annas and then, after that, to the house of Caiaphas, where Mark's Gospel seems to suggest the trial took place; Matthew echoes this while Luke actually cites the High Priest's house. The writer then asked what happened. The witness told the writer what had happened without saying where it had taken place, so the writer assumed, wrongly, that the reported events had happened in the house of Annas and not in the House of Caiaphas, the High Priest: everything was recorded as happening in the wrong house. The witness, being illiterate, will not have known that a mistake was being made. The crucial point is that the witnessing disciple was known in and had access to the house of the High Priest, and was probably not known, at least not favourably, in that of Annas. Thus he is almost certain to have been unable to report at first hand the goings-on in the house of Annas. This is one of the clearest pieces of evidence of dual authorship and how the Gospel came to be written down. Clearest of all, however, is the difference between the ending of chapter 20 and the ending of chapter 21. The ending of chapter 20 is clearly the writer saying that he has left out many of the signs that Jesus had produced, but that he had provided these selected ones to demonstrate that Jesus was divine and showing us the true way to God. He was providing very firm evidence for us all to believe in the truth of that message. But the difference between this ending and the ending of chapter 21 is dazzling. The ending of chapter 21 is clearly from a completely unsophisticated, totally naive witness, not the learned theologian writer, and he was witnessing to what Jesus had done, rather than provided as signs, which was the aim of the writer. We see the stark difference between the two minds, when we compare the academic restraint in the last verse of chapter 20 with the unbridled exuberance in the last verse of chapter 21, where the witness says that if all that Jesus had done were to be written down, he supposed the whole world would not have enough room for all the books that would have to be written. At the same time this shows how much of his time the witness had spent with Jesus. There are two totally different minds at work, one far better educated than the other, but the uneducated one possessing information of such overwhelming importance that his input was included even when it was contrary to the beliefs of the writer. Only the all-consuming interest in Jesus will have made two such strikingly different minds co-operate to produce what may be the most important book in the Bible. It becomes clear too, that the last chapter was almost essential for establishing the proof of the truth of the information given in the last Gospel, as well as providing further evidence of Jesus's reappearance after the crucifixion. It also casts an interesting light on the slightly tardy start to the preaching of the message of Jesus.

Now that something has been established about the witness, it might be helpful if one were able to work out how the witness had come to see so much. Someone so young (too young to be considered a full disciple) and illiterate, must have been extremely energetic, as well as endowed with insatiable childlike curiosity, to have discovered so much. He had seen a man who had been partially blind since birth having his full sight being given him, and then the confrontation between the healed man and the High Priest's council. He had witnessed a conversation between Jesus and a woman from Samaria and then heard her exclamations to her fellow townsfolk when she went back to fetch her current partner. His outrunning the very impulsive and enthusiastic Peter to the tomb on the morning of the disappearance of Jesus's body shows that he was a very good, indeed probably habitual, runner. In chapter 11 he was in all the important places when the different meetings occurred between various characters, with it all culminating with Jesus summoning Lazarus out of his coma and out of the tomb with his stentorian voice. For instance, when the writer says that Martha told her sister Mary 'secretly' that Jesus had come and that she was wanted by him, it will have been by signals and possibly mouthed but unspoken words that the witness had seen for himself.

John, the witness, was an undemonstrative, unassuming sort of person, which may have been why Jesus gave him and his presumably like-minded brother the name Boanerges (Sons of Thunder). Jesus showed the same sense of humour when he nicknamed the supremely impulsive Simon 'Peter' (Rock). We know the witness was a very modest sort of person from Luke's account of him with Peter in Acts of the Apostles, where John never speaks. Interestingly, Paul, in his letter to the Galatians 2:9, says that John was reputed to be a pillar of the Church, along with James, the brother of Jesus, who was the leader of the Church in Jerusalem, rather than the brother of John, the witness, one assumes, and Cephas (Peter) when these three gave their right hand of fellowship for Paul and Barnabas to go and preach to the Gentiles, while they went to preach to the Jews (the circumcised). We know the witness never promoted himself in the material which he supplied to the writer of the Gospel. We also gather, from Luke's Acts as well as from the Gospels, that he was a constant companion and very close confidant of Simon Peter. This is most clearly demonstrated when Peter wanted to know, during the Last Supper, who was going to betray Jesus. The enquiry from Peter will have been by signals, so small and so brief as to be almost imperceptible, and the reply will have been similar. No one else will have noticed what was going on. His very quiet charm probably endeared the boy to the High Priest and all his household, who will certainly have known about his association with Jesus. This knowledge, that the witness associated with Jesus, was made clear when the maid, who had just let Peter in at the request of the witness, immediately suggested to Peter that he must be a follower of Jesus too, thus eliciting the first of the three denials.

With the establishment of the reliability of the witness, his memories being unfaded and almost undistorted, the physical appearance of Jesus may usefully be addressed. Early images of Jesus represented him as about one and a half metres tall, stooping, continuous eyebrows, long-nosed and ugly. He is likely to have had an easily identifiable silhouette as his form was recognised, when it was dark, by frightened disciples – they had thought it was his ghost – when they were crossing the Sea of Galilee in a storm-tossed boat. Then there are the words attributed to Jesus by Luke: "No doubt you will quote the saying, 'Physician, heal thyself.' " His disabilities will have been clearly visible. Then there is the prophecy in Isaiah, chapter 53, about Jesus being deformed; it is felt by many that this prophecy is about Jesus specifically and not about the state of the children of Israel in general. His unfavourable appearance and deformity, which would have been attributed to some sin or sins, would not have hastened his appearance in public life. It is very interesting that Isaiah says that he made his grave (crucifixion) with the wicked – the two 'criminals' on either side – and with a rich man, foreshadowing the new, still unused tomb to which Joseph of Arimathea and Nicodemus, each of whom may be presumed rich, took his body and then anointed it.

Next, the very special abilities of Jesus could usefully be assessed and outlined. Many of us may have met people with almost incredible telepathic powers. There was one, Hanina ben (son of) Dosa, who lived a short while after Jesus, who is said to have healed the son of Gamaliel, reportedly Paul's teacher, just by praying for him. Hanina said he could tell from the fluency in his prayer if the patient would recover or not: telepathic power. The telepathic sensitivity of Jesus must have been enormously more powerful. Exorcism was commonly practised at the time and Jesus would have been outstanding at that too. His healing hands were so good that he was adjudged a sorcerer, as well as leading the people of Israel astray with false teaching; this is according to the Babylonian Talmud which states he was hung (crucified) on the eve of the Passover for these crimes.

TWO

—

A BRIEF BIOGRAPHY OF JESUS

In this chapter there are changes to the order of events in the story of Jesus which have been deduced from the very significant omissions in John's version of Jesus's life. John assumes that Jesus had been born quite normally, quite naturally to his father and mother. He will have known about the birth and childhood stories in Matthew and Luke but significantly omits any reference to them. He will have known about the temptation but just as significantly omits any mention of that. Why should one expect God's direct representative, let alone God, to be tempted anyway? He must have been tested *before* he was entrusted with God's mission on earth. He does not mention the Transfiguration. These points are dealt with in chapter 6. However, a brief biographical summary might take this shape. Jesus was born to Mary and Joseph. However, just as it is impossible to know if God influenced any of the human decisions in the last world war that led to defeat of the evil that was the satanic Nazi regime in Germany, we cannot know if God organised the right man, Jesus, to be born in the right place, at the right time and with all the abilities and qualities that were needed for his purpose. Jesus will have grown up in the shadow of the unremarkable family's workshop, in which he probably began working as soon as he was able to do so. The family is likely to have been well-to-do, as it ran a joinery business connected with building. There is, however, no mention of hired servants. It would appear that Jesus may have had some visible disability or disfigurement, as has been pointed out, which does not seem to have impaired his ability to work or move about. This disability is written of, as has been said, by Isaiah in chapter 53, vv. 2-4, and alluded to by Luke in chapter 4, v. 23, where he makes Jesus say, quoting, one surmises, one of many lost passages from Ecclesiasticus, Πάντως ἐρεῖτέ μοι τὴν παραβολὴν ταύτην: ἰατρέ, θεράπευσον σεαυτόν, "Doubtless, you will say to me this (as a) comparison, 'Physician, heal thyself.'" This suggests that Jesus did indeed suffer from a visible disability, as Isaiah seems to be prophesying.

One should bear in mind that where the personality is particularly powerful, other attributes, such as a physical imperfection, are less likely to be noticed consciously. A magnetically moving face, accompanied by an irresistible voice, attracts the eyes to that and away from everything else.

It is possible that he was the chief worker in the family business and met many people during his work. As a result of this regular contact he came to realise the extent of his almost preternatural abilities to heal, understand others telepathically and to influence them. Luke says that Jesus started his ministry when he was about 30 years old; such a claim has no material effect on what Luke is trying to prove about Jesus, so it will be an unbiassed genuine belief gathered from the evidence available when he wrote the Gospel. So we may guess that it might be that at about 30 years of age Jesus left his home and the business to go into the wilderness. He felt he needed to think about his endowments and what he should do with them, so as to improve the conditions of the ordinary person: he was driven by compassionate love for oppressed people. This was the Temptation (covered again in chapter 6). Should he become a renowned healer, or an entertainer to lift the spirits of the people, or a leader to free Judaea from the Romans, as the Maccabees had freed Israel 150 years earlier? At what turned out to be the end of the Temptation, he was led by the Spirit to John the Baptist and induced to be baptised by him. This electrifying experience resulted in God taking over at that moment and directing him. He remained human but became God's special agent. His knowledge of the Scriptures was such as one would *not* expect of a Galilean artisan, however regularly he may have attended the synagogue, but inspiration from God would account for this. It is obvious that Jesus, as God's direct agent and representative, was performing a precise function that no human had performed before and which no human has performed since.

His immediate family, seeing him leave his job in the successful and relatively important family business, would have felt badly let down and be wondering what had got into their previously normal brother. When he cleansed the Temple, they will have thought that a demon had taken possession of him, so they tried, unsuccessfully, to take him out of public life to save the family's reputation. This attempt to take Jesus out of public life is referred to in Mark 3:20 and vv.31-35 of the same chapter, where a valid reason for thinking he had gone out of his mind *just is not there*. It is much more likely that the cleansing of the Temple will have been the reason for their thinking he had gone out of his mind. Similarly, later on, his immediate family, his brothers (John chapter 7), told him to go to the Feast of Tabernacles, where the wording of the story makes it clear that they hoped Jesus would make such a fool of himself that his public life would be finished. He did go a little later, but they were mistaken. His ministry continued unabated and ended with his crucifixion, fulfilling, to a remarkable extent, the prophecy in the 53rd chapter of Isaiah. But, however well sourced the inspiration from God, one cannot expect a human mind, even the writer of this part of Isaiah, to get every single point right. All the same, its detail is close enough to be connected with Jesus by everyone except the most determined doubters.

It is clear that Jesus had a strong but gentle sense of humour and was determined to talk and deal with anyone whom he might meet, regardless of Jewish tradition and teaching. It is clear, too, that he had a very powerful sense of truth and justice and an even more powerful driving love for his fellow-man, particularly the young. His sense of injustice was highlighted at the time when he overturned the tables of the money changers and victim sellers in the Temple because of their inordinate exploitation of innocent worshippers coming to discharge the sacrificial duties imposed on them by the Law. The legal money in the Temple was Jewish money, but the money in normal use was Roman, so the money changers charged very high exchange rates so as to make money for themselves and for the High Priests. Those inspecting the sacrificial offerings – and they made a significant charge for this – which had been brought by the worshippers were, for the same reasons, determined to find faults and staggeringly high prices were demanded (about 19 times in the case of doves as compared with that charged outside the Temple) for the sacrificial offerings on sale, which, of course, were deemed to be up to standard. It is possible that any loose change in Temple money may often have been put into the trumpets (receptacles) for general offerings in the Temple, of which there were six, another seven being for specific purposes such as upkeep of the Temple. These trumpets were situated against a wall in the shelter of a colonnade in the Court of the Women; they were narrow at the top and swelling out towards the foot.

Jesus was particularly concerned about how the innumerable ramifications of the Jewish Law restricted sensible behaviour. He was disgusted at the overweening power of the interpreters of the Law who were always enforcing ever more impractical, nitpicking detail. For instance, a Sabbath day's journey – a journey was considered by the Law to be work – was defined as about 1,000 yards from one's home. Some bright sparks, though, came up with the idea of having food depots a thousand yards from their homes, which depots also counted as home, so that they could travel three times as far, quite legally, on the Sabbath. Indeed, sometimes a whole municipality was very cunningly defined as a single home, so that any of its inhabitants could legally travel 1,000 yards outside the town's boundaries on the Sabbath. The bureaucracy behind the Law was impersonal, heartless and self-serving. The Law should have existed to help, not hinder people. Jesus knew people did not exist for the sole purpose of observing and maintaining the Law. In fact, Jesus saw Jews as slaves to the Law and its administrators. He came to free them from that and to show that the only real way to save the human race from distress was to demonstrate that it was deep interpersonal love that would heal every human quarrel. The Law was meant to help and guide, not to rule without regard to common sense.

One might note, in passing, the bond between the witness disciple and Jesus, which will have owed more to the disciple's adoration of Jesus than to Jesus's love for him; Jesus's affection will have been more like that of a teacher's caring love for a young pupil, as a good group leader cannot wisely afford to display any special preference for a member of his group. It is this bond that will have made him such a trustworthy witness.

The effect of Jesus's teaching on his increasing number of followers was too extensive and powerful to be tolerated by the authorities, centred in the High Priest's entourage and the Sanhedrin. Jesus's teaching was contrary to what the authorities wanted Jews to believe. It was heretical, therefore, and deemed to be coming from a false prophet. Such behaviour was a capital offence. It was decided that Jesus had to be killed, but that his followers were not so numerous or dangerous that they should be killed too. He was duly sacrificed on the cross by the Romans to keep the peace. As has been made clear by several historians, the Jews were not particularly peaceable in the religious jungle of that time, while the 'Pax Romana' was a cardinal tenet in the rulers' minds. The execution of just one man to maintain that peace seemed reasonable and wise.

Among the crowd watching the crucifixion were Jesus's mother and the young witness disciple. It is just possible that Joseph of Arimathea and Nicodemus were not far from the scene, as they were involved in taking down the body, anointing it and its entombment.

Very early on the first day of the week, Mary Magdalene went to the tomb to visit her beloved Master. She was astonished to find that the stone which had been sealing the tomb had been rolled away and that the body was not there. She ran to tell Simon Peter and the witness what had happened. Their investigation revealed relatively undisturbed winding cloths, as if the body might have disappeared in a case of something like spontaneous human combustion. They left, but Mary must have returned and suffered what may have been an hallucination, organised by God. She thought she saw two angels where the body had been. She then recognised neither the form nor the voice of the risen Jesus when she turned away from the tomb. She thought she was talking to the gardener. She was told not to touch him, suggesting that her experience was like that of encountering a ghost whose real body was not there.

Following this, Jesus is revealed in similar fashion, coming and going as if in a dream, to a number of those who had known him well, so that what had been a totally dispirited and frightened band started energetically and very successfully to spread the message of Jesus. As they were illiterate we do not know what they said unless it is reported by Luke in 'Acts'. We know, however, that the message of Jesus was spread with amazing speed, and as far as Rome. The wonderful tradition that Thomas took the Gospel to India is good enough to be true.

THREE

—

JESUS'S ROLE AND MESSAGE

The Jews were so taken up with atonement for sins that a lamb was sacrificed every day in the Temple for this, even during times of starvation or siege, until the Temple was destroyed in 70 AD. This Jewish belief in the importance of atonement may have led to overemphasis of the idea that Jesus was taking away the sin of the world. It might be argued rather that he was showing how positive acts and beneficent behaviour bring 'salvation' to everyone. We may talk of our needing goodwill at Christmas time, but Jesus was talking about our needing it all the time, not just during a short season of the year. The kingdom we refer to in the Lord's Prayer is one in which we all behave as beings theoretically behave in Heaven, but here on earth. It is the kingdom foretold by Isaiah 11:1-9 where Jesus is the founder of the new kingdom of love and universal goodwill. Everyone on earth should realise that God is the loving creator Father to whom Jesus, as our signpost, is showing us the way. We are to show that we love God as we should in our determination to cultivate goodwill for everyone, even when we may hate, or be repelled by, what is done. This is the commandment given so often at the end of John's Gospel, particularly when Jesus is credited with saying that everyone will be able to see they are his disciples when they display goodwill for one another. The kingdom we pray for is one of universal goodwill. We should also show our love for God by looking after the World and all that is in it as well as we are able. Climate activists and champions of the life of flora and fauna should welcome this, and Buddhists might do so too.

Jesus was showing us, as well, that confining our care and attention to those who are part and parcel of our own local societies and lives was not what he was teaching: we are to care for everyone, regardless of race, belief or culture – or of anything else for that matter.

A world in which absolutely everyone is determined to cultivate universal goodwill will not be plagued by any more destructive quarrelling; the results of human work and effort will not be wantonly wasted on purpose any more. This is a far more comfortable world than the present one. Fully accepting Jesus's version of how we should believe in God, and behave accordingly, can bring this wonderful new world into existence. The obviously timeless, universal common sense of Jesus's message shows that it must have come from God, while it is easily intelligible to almost anyone, anywhere. There are those who cannot travel to prescribed destinations, whether because of physical condition or geographical situation; there are some who live so far north or so far south that solar-time based rules cannot reasonably be expected to be applied. Christianity, on the other hand, is for absolutely everyone, anywhere, of any sort, of any ability, whether paralysed or blind or deaf – for how can someone who is deaf and blind, as well as possibly dumb, hear, adequately learn or recite holy texts, or even always be able to travel safely to distant lands?

It may be more than evidence for a factual basis that is wanted. The teaching matters too. It might be noticed that the teaching of Jesus was carried out for everyone there at that time to see. It was not based on visions but on direction from God at the actual moment of delivery, witnessed by many, not just a favoured few. The accounts of the teaching of Jesus are totally intelligible in any translation, in any language. They do not have to be uttered or intoned in a special way; they do not have to be memorised; they do not require actions that cannot be carried out by anyone and everyone in all circumstances. The parables in the first three Gospels are so constructed, so easy to remember, that no special exercises in rote learning are needed, nor should they be. We show love for God in what we do, above all, not in what we may have managed to learn by heart. Incidentally, there are people who are mentally disadvantaged, who cannot learn extensive strings of words by heart. Jesus's Judaism is for everyone, not just those who faithfully commit great tracts of script to memory.

We can take a line from what we may be sure about in the other Gospels. We may be relatively sure of the truth of whatever is completely in agreement with what Jesus shows us in the stories in the Gospel of John, so long as we can see that it is not what the writer of John or the writers of the other Gospels are at all likely to have invented to fill up their accounts. We might think of the parable of the Good Samaritan, which tells us we should be concerned for anyone whom we may find in trouble and that we should not allow laws of cleanliness or any suchlike to dissuade us from helping. We might think of the parable of the talents which tells us that whatever we have, whether material possessions or knowledge or mental understanding and expertise or anything else, should be used for helping others or sharing with them, so that they may benefit too. We are not intended to keep whatever we have to ourselves and so benefit no one else at all. We might think of the parable of the sheep and the goats, where anyone who shows loving concern for his fellow man when he finds that person in difficulties, even demeaning circumstances, is fulfilling God's will for us all. We might think of the parable of the Prodigal Son where forgiveness for the most selfish of sins is shown to be right when the transgressor repents completely and genuinely, and also how a transgressor may come to repent. We might think of how it is said to be difficult for a rich man to enter the Kingdom of Heaven, the wealth of the rich man being material possessions, or academic knowledge, political power or military might that distracts the possessor from loving and caring for a neighbour in the way that one should. Jesus does not teach that God has created any of us so that we may be subjected to eternal punishment; he certainly does not teach us that the fuel for the outdated idea of eternal fires in hell would be human transgressors of God's laws and ordinances. A loving, compassionate, merciful father would never create such a thing as an eternal hell for any of his beloved creation, nor deliberately lead astray any unbeliever so that eternal punishment would then be ordained for that person. The teaching of Jesus has come straight from God, under God's direction, and is timeless.

An example of the timelessness may be found in the Lord's Prayer, Matthew 6:9-13 and Luke 11:2-4, although it does not appear in Mark or John's Gospel. The

'Our Father' beginning shows that God is for everyone. 'Hallowed be thy name' reminds us that not only should we *not* use God's name in thoughtless exclamations but also that, when we do use God's name, we should be completely involved, completely committed, not tepid or half-hearted. The 'Thy Kingdom come' plus the 'Thy will be done as it is in Heaven' are prayers that we should all behave towards one another with determined goodwill, just as Jesus has taught us. 'Give us this day our daily bread' is quite obviously asking that what is essential for a true spiritual life may be among our experiences that day, even if those experiences are painful. 'Forgive us as we forgive others' is self-explanatory and reminds us that an unforgiving state of mind is a destructive pain for the possessor; we are all much more comfortable when we hold no grudges against anyone else, although we may need God's help in finding out how to manage to forgive. 'Lead us not into temptation' might remind us of Oscar Wilde saying that he could resist anything except temptation, but we are still begging that we may not be tested beyond our breaking point and that we may be inspired to do good. 'Deliver us from evil' is begging that we may be able to resist the temptation to do anything that results in evil and that we may not come under the influence of the devil.

There may be no really obvious parables in John's Gospel, such as appear in the other Gospels, but it is possible to read many of the chapters as if they have parabolic messages. Even in the first chapter, when John and Andrew decide to follow Jesus, prompted by John the Baptist, we have a possible example, as the pair stop following the latest popular fad of the time and follow God's newly appointed special agent instead. 'Do not be sidelined into pursuing what is no more than the latest popular attraction when what is real, good, true and healthy is now available to be attended to, a true light to help us all see and understand better what we are meant to do in this world, for the management of which God has given us the responsibility.' We may remember, at the same time, that at the moment of baptism, when God takes over, Jesus is completely Jewish, a complete believer in the Judaic traditions and basic teaching. He always remained steadfastly a proper Jew, although he came to know, if he did not already, that Judaism needed to be refashioned. As Isaiah made clear, in 2:2 for instance, the Jewish faith is due to be established in every country and among every people on earth, so it has to be intelligible and acceptable everywhere in the world. It might be right if we think of what we now call 'Christianity' as rather more Jesus's version of Judaism than just 'Christianity'. Exactly as John Wesley did not want to think of himself as leaving the Church of England, so Jesus never gave up being a Jew: he was fulfilling the Law, not abolishing it; he was preaching a new form of Judaism. Nevertheless, it might be more helpful if one understood that he was getting rid of the pernickety additional material, the distracting decorations, added by the bureaucratic scribes and their ilk, making it clear that the only fundamental law that matters is showing love for one's creator God by loving other people, wanting to help them and looking after the rest of his creation. Another consideration is that the idea of the Messiah (anointed one) was a human function, connected with establishing Jewish salvation and political dominance, whereas Jesus was much more than that. He was God's agent in a way that no one else has ever been, and had been *made man* to give God's message to every people on earth, not just the Jews. This message is not tied to any one language or the people of that language; it is not tied to any one place or area; it does not betray outdated modes of thinking or culture; its ideas translate with their full meaning into any language and so can be understood and followed in every culture that may be encountered, past or present.

FOUR

ACCOUNTS WHICH ARE TOO TRUE TO LIFE TO HAVE BEEN INVENTED AND THE FIRST SIX SIGNS PERFORMED BY JESUS, CHOSEN BY THE WRITER TO SHOW HIS MESSAGE CAME FROM GOD

When John the Presbyter had heard enough from the newly discovered witness, the youngest son of Zebedee, to know that writing a new Gospel was his pressing duty, but before he started writing, he must have decided that the structural theme of his work would be seven signs, seven being a most special number in the eyes of the Jews. The first sign was the apparent turning of water into wine at the wedding in Cana in Galilee. Jesus made it clear that this apparently miraculous sign could not be produced exactly when his mother said it was needed. This suggests that more time might have been necessary for psychological preparation by means of the telepathic power of Jesus for the 'miracle' to work. This is a parable too: the effect of Jesus can change the dullest, most ordinary of things into exciting and useful experiences.

Throughout the Gospel there is frequent reference to 'The Jews' as if they are to be regarded as enemies of Jesus. It might be possible that the attitudes of John the writer had been shaped by previous incidents and that his antipathy to particular Jews in authority had become generalised, so that he felt animosity against all Jews, when it might have been more appropriate if he had reserved his ill-will for the particular ones who had, as he clearly thought, treated Jesus, Paul and him unacceptably. There was clearly a healthy number of Jews who favoured Jesus very strongly, else he would not have survived as long as he did.

At the time of the baptism the descent of the dove on Jesus is related, although not the baptism itself, which one assumes preceded the occurrence. One might have expected this to be one of the seven signs selected by the writer to demonstrate Jesus's divine status, but this was not witnessed by the informant and so may have been considered insufficiently attested to be given as one of them. Very important, however, is the recruitment of the first five disciples, particularly as the details of the recruitment more or less establish that this account of how they came to be disciples is clearly the right one. We have, first, John the Baptist suggesting to two of his disciples that they would be better off following Jesus rather than him. Jesus's asking them what they were trying to find out and their spending the rest of the day with him make it clear that this really happened. Andrew, Simon's brother, turns out to be one of the first two disciples of Jesus. He *first* (or early next morning) goes to find his brother, Simon, with words we cannot be sure were actually heard by the witness. These words may have been calculated by the writer, but, whatever Andrew said, they will have expressed very considerable admiration for Jesus and appreciation of the importance of his message. The decision of Jesus to nickname someone as impulsive as Simon, 'The Rock' (Peter), shows both the rapidity with which Jesus summed people up but also his sense of humour. His naming of Simon as 'Simon, son of John' may well have been due to telepathic command rather than previously provided information.

We have the first recruit who was actually chosen

by Jesus named as Philip. We are told he came from *Bethsaida, the 'city' of Andrew and Peter.* The writer is most unlikely to have known this before nor will he have have invented it. It can come only from an informant, the witness. Further confirmation of the firsthand status is the fact that Philip then went to find Nathanael. This might be the disciple named Bartholomew in the other Gospels and Acts. None of this will be novelistic contrivance. We have the Sherlock Holmes style deduction on the part of Jesus, when he had just seen the sun-dazzled eyes of Nathanael, that Nathanael was a studious sort of person and that he had been reading or meditating or praying under a fig tree, the cool place of peace. This all goes to show that the event actually happened. We have had Nathanael asking whether anything good could be expected to come from Nazareth. There is no theological reason for including this piece of information. To have invented it is both quite outside the novelist skills of the writer – if he had any – and quite out of tune with his declared devotion to divine truth and reality. He put it in because he realised, the moment he heard this little vignette, that it would authenticate the account that he was giving, which was being harvested from the information provided by the witness about Jesus's life and ministry. The proofs of the remarkable quality of witness and the truth of the events recorded in this Gospel are being displayed from the very beginning.

Perhaps one of the most important signs not in the writer's list is the evidence to be deduced from the fact that John the Baptist told Andrew and John that they should be following Jesus rather than him. John the Baptist seems to have been a very powerful figure and such figures are more likely to promote themselves rather than others. This is evidence indeed suggesting that Jesus is a far, far more important figure than anyone else has ever been or ever will be.

The signs are the backbone of the case being presented by the writer. The signs have been identified as *first*, turning water into wine in chapter 2, *second*, the healing of the courtier's boy at the end of chapter 4, *third*, the healing of the paralytic at the pool of Bethzatha, in the first part of chapter 5, *fourth*, the feeding of the five thousand in the first part of chapter 6, *fifth*, the healing of the man born partially blind in chapter 9, *sixth*, the raising of Lazarus in chapter 11, which was by far the strongest reason for the authorities wanting Jesus silenced permanently, *seventh*, a double sign, the strongest and final sign, the crucifixion and resurrection, all detailed in the last three chapters, 19-21. This last double sign, being fully attested by the amount and strength of the witness that exists to confirm its truth, is so strong and powerful as to be more or less irrefutable. To think otherwise would suggest that wilful blindness is at work. This last sign is as good as final proof of the validity of the Gospel's message as delivered by Jesus, even though the precise style will have been shaped by the theology of the writer.

The first sign signifies that Jesus can make every moment of life seem worthwhile; the second shows that Jesus brings spiritual healing; the third shows us that Jesus frees us from the spiritual paralysis which may keep us from acting publicly as followers of Jesus; the fourth sign shows that Jesus has spiritual food for every single one of us; the fifth sign shows that Jesus offers us spiritual sight; the sixth sign shows that Jesus offers spiritual life while the seventh sign is the seal of the truth and power of the whole promise.

But however we look at things, none of us should ever be deterred, as we are all in different positions and so have to work out our own individual paths to the truth of God. We are able to do this with the aid of the light we find in the pages of this Gospel and the other writings in the Bible, which will illuminate our way. Even though we die, we have made ripples during our lives, sometimes great, sometimes tiny, and we should try to ensure that the ripples we make and so leave behind us are as beneficial as possible.

The theology of the writer may be wonderful but it does not provide a contemporary picture of Jesus's character nor a reliable representation of his preaching. The stories which may be assigned to the witness most readily, are those that can be singled out by noting exactly what it is that makes them obviously different from what is more clearly the teaching and theological explanation of the writer. The life-like pictures of Jesus and his disciples are shown only in the stories. It is these life-like pictures of Jesus and his ministry that matter more than anything else in establishing the truth of Jesus's life and teaching; it is these pictures which are as good as living proofs of the ministry of Jesus taking place and its being directed by God; using these stories as a yardstick, we can work out what is credible in the other writings in the Bible, both Old and New Testaments. We then have a trustworthy picture of Jesus and can assess more accurately what we may believe he is likely to have taught.

The first sign chosen happened at the wedding in Cana in Galilee, near Nazareth. There will have been only five disciples at this stage, but they seem to have been invited along with Jesus's mother and Jesus. Joseph is not mentioned so we may deduce that he is likely to have died. Jesus, presumably the eldest son, had probably become the main worker in the family joinery business, and would have remained so until his departure to start his ministry. Before turning water into wine, we have Mary, Jesus's mother, telling him that they had run out of wine. This shows that she knew something of his 'magical' abilities and was hoping Jesus would do something about it. There is no evidence yet that the family thought he had gone off the rails. Jesus explained that it was not the right moment yet, but this did not deter Mary who then went and instructed the servants there to do whatever Jesus might tell them to do. If the miracle was brought about by Jesus making everyone there think it was wine when it was only water, the delay is perfectly explained, as Jesus needed to have exactly the right moment successfully to exercise his powers. The Jewish custom of mixing wine with a great deal of water before serving may be important for a full understanding of how this 'miracle' may have worked.

Following the first sign, the transformation of the wine, we have the cleansing of the Temple, when Jesus drove out all the larger animals and overturned the tables of the money changers. The making of a lash of cords to drive out the larger animals, combined with the other detail, supports the probability of the information about this episode coming from the witness. Particularly interesting is the following interchange. Jesus said, speaking of his body, when they thought that he was talking about the Temple, that they should go ahead and destroy it and that he would raise it up again in three days. With a likely reference to this, Mark writes of Jesus being accused of saying that he would raise up a temple not built with hands in three days (14:58). They mockingly pointed out that it had taken 46 years to restore the Temple so that made Jesus's claim that he would raise it up again in three days appear pretty ridiculous. Jesus, of course, with his customary use of the unexpected, was referring to his own body which 'they' were destined to kill. The restoration of the Temple had started in 19 BC, so 46 years later was 28 AD (there was no year 0). If the crucifixion was two years later that would put its date at 30 AD, fitting the calculation of the famous Jewish scholar, Geza Vermes. A passover followed soon after the cleansing and Jesus was crucified at the time of the third; so there was one Passover in between this one and the last.

The cleansing is *not* one of the events chosen to be a sign, even though it might have been interpreted as a sign of Jesus 'cleaning up' the Judaic religious system, as well as himself becoming the sacrificial victim: he was the only 'large' one left. This might well be because it was taken as a sign by his immediate family that Jesus was now out of his mind, possessed by a demon, while it was not considered to be a sign that contributed to the demonstration that Jesus was divine. Indeed, this was very probably the event that persuaded Jesus's family that they needed to take Jesus out of public life, as Mark's writer recounted in chapter 3:20 & vv.31-33. An additional consideration is that this was the furthest a Gentile was allowed to go into the Temple, and this court was supposed to be available for prayer. How might a Gentile be expected to be able to pray properly, surrounded by such a hubbub?

Next, in chapter 3, we have the meeting between Jesus and Nicodemus.The meeting took place when there were no followers to be impressed by the importance that seemed now to be attached to Jesus by the authorities. Nicodemus was an important member of the Sanhedrin, the supreme religious court of the Jews, presided over by the High Priest. The early use of the phrase 'Truly, truly' suggests that the witness was not at the actual meeting but was told about it afterwards; the quantity and style of didactic material would appear to support this version of events. Jesus probably explained to the witness not long after, perhaps the next day, what had happened, in this fashion possibly: "Yesterday evening, an important member of the Sanhedrin, Nicodemus, came to question me to find out if what I was telling people amounted to false teaching. I was able to show him that my teaching, which I outlined to him, was in fact in accordance with the law and the prophets, so he went away without discovering anything to lay before my would-be accusers in the Sanhedrin. I am afraid that some of the things which I said, I said in a way he did not understand straightaway, as people remember things much better when they have to make a real effort to understand what one is trying to put across. For instance, I spoke about needing to be born again; of course I meant it spiritually, but he took it literally, as I knew he would; but he knew exactly what I meant by the time I had finished. He's secretly on our side now."

Next comes the questioning of John the Baptist about purification, raised by an unnamed Jew and

John's disciples, and the concern that Jesus's followers were baptising more people than John was. The style of the theological pronouncements is what one would expect from the writer rather than from the witness, although the event itself seems to have been covered in the witness's account, as the subsequent decisions of Jesus are explained by the fact that this meeting was reported to the Pharisees, who would have passed the information straightaway to the High Priest and other authorities. A further confirmation that this came from the witness is the correction: the writer had said first that it was Jesus who was baptising, and then realised, after further questioning, that it was Jesus's disciples who were actually baptising, and not Jesus himself. Writing, then, was a laborious task and paper relatively expensive: one wasted neither effort nor expense, so our writer would not have rewritten everything.

As a result of this information reaching the authorities we have the amazing encounter with the woman from Samaria. The group had taken the quickest and so safest route to Galilee, instead of the round-about route that Jews would normally take so as to avoid going through Samaria. Samaritans claimed both descent from Ephraim and Manasseh and that they kept the proper Mosaic religion, following the first five books of the Bible. However, Israel had been conquered by Assyria in 722 BC and, according to Josephus, the Jewish historian, foreign peoples had been forcibly settled in Samaria and there had been intermarriage as a result. Jews were not supposed to marry people who were not Jews. To make matters worse, the Samaritans' special temple on Mount Gerizim had been destroyed by the High Priest, John Hyrcanus, in about 110 BC. It is clear that in the time of Jesus, Samaritans and the rest of the Jews were just about as hostile and rigidly intolerant of each other as Roman Catholics and Protestants in Northern Ireland once were.

The encounter with the woman from Samaria, though it is not given as a sign, is not only unique but also very illuminating, because it demonstrates, as foretold by Isaiah, that the God of the Jews will be the God for every people on earth, even for those considered utterly despised outcasts, such as the Samaritans, not just for the chosen children of Israel. A detail which more or less confirms the authenticity of the story is the obvious impatience of the disciples, who have gone to some trouble to obtain food for Jesus, when Jesus did not eat the food when they offered it. Even more indicative of the truth of the story is the disciples asking, quite naturally, if someone else has given Jesus something to eat, as Jesus must have said something about having what one imagines would be spiritual food, as spoken of in the Lord's Prayer. It is interesting that the witness had not gone with the other disciples; he might have been too young to consider himself a proper disciple, while his all-conquering interest will have kept him with Jesus anyway.

Further confirmation of Jesus's telepathic powers is the extent of the knowledge of the woman's past and present circumstances that he now has. He amazes her, initially, when he, a Jewish man, speaks to a woman, which custom did not allow, and to a woman from Samaria on top of that, which was considered even less becoming or appropriate. Men were not supposed to speak even to their wives in public. When, having asked for a drink, he told her that he had special water, drinking which would quench thirst for ever, Jesus used a word that could mean 'living and spiritual' or 'running'. She took it that he meant running water, so she probably thought he was half-witted, pointing out that without any container which he could let down into the well, he could not possibly get any water. She went on to ask mockingly for this wonderful water which Jesus was offering her, so he suggested she should go and get her husband. At this she jeeringly retorted that she did not have a husband, whereupon Jesus astounded her by revealing that he knew everything about her already. She very suddenly realised that this extraordinary man was so far ahead of her that her contempt for him was vaporised in a flash.

It is clear that the conversation went on for a long time as it lasted nearly all the time that the disciples needed to go to obtain and bring back the food from Sychar, which would have been about a mile away if

Jacob's well was at the foot of Mount Gerizim. This is likely as Jesus must have been pointing to this holy site in his conversation when he said that Samaritans would not be worshipping on '*this*' mountain nor in Jerusalem either. Incidentally, the dismissal of Jerusalem as a place of worship implies, one might think, that Jesus is foreseeing the worldwide adoption of the Jewish faith in the new form which was being preached by him. Jerusalem and the site of the Temple might remain the most important holy place for ethnic Jews, but would not be the focal point for the new worldwide form of Judaism. The centre for worshipping God is the world, not one small restricted site, nor any particular building, such as St Peter's, Rome.

We can tell the woman's thinking was now completely dominated by Jesus: she even forgot her water container and left it behind in her enthusiasm to tell everyone else in Sychar about her new found hero. The woman was almost certainly a well-known local personality because the people there were deeply impressed with what she said; they asked Jesus to stay there two more days and then, after that, said they were now even more convinced of the importance of his message as they had heard it straight from Jesus for themselves.

The latter part of the chapter, which deals with the second sign, the healing of the courtier's son, is introduced with another little detail that the truth-dedicated writer of the Gospel would not have invented.

The occurrence of this detail also adds strength to the proposition that the Gospel was being written down while the writer was questioning the witness. The writer knows, from the first three Gospels, that Jesus had spoken about a prophet being without honour in his own country and so began this part with a statement to that effect, only to discover from the witness that the people there, contrary to all expectations except those of Jesus, had heard about Jesus's recent exploits and so were very receptive to him and his ideas: Jesus *did* have honour there. This detail is strong evidence that the Gospel was being written down as the writer acquired the information from the witness.

In the euphoric atmosphere surrounding Jesus, the possibly Gentile courtier desperately asks that his son be healed. Jesus, in complete rapport with the crowd and occasion, jokes about them all wanting 'wonders' when the courtier makes his entreaty. Jesus will have said this in a way that caused neither offence nor occasion for doubt on the part of the courtier. Then, so reassuring will have been the tone of Jesus's voice when he said his son would be quite all right, the courtier had complete faith that everything would go well. The statement that the healing occurred at the appropriate time for a fever being cured suggests that the ending of the story may not have been supplied by the witness but calculated by the writer.

Chapter 5 now starts with the third sign, which might be a parabolic representation of Israel as all the sick people around the pool, waiting for a new prophet to come and stir the spiritual waters so that they could be healed. The detailed description of the site, a foretaste of the novelist of today expertly setting the scene, suggests strongly a witness's vivid memories. However, the actual number given to explain how long the paralytic had suffered from his disease, suggests input from the writer rather than from the witness, as the number 38 could be taken to represent the number of years the Israelites were supposed to have wandered in the wilderness before they entered the promised land, or even the number of centuries they were to wait for the Messiah to arrive. It would seem likely that the paralytic was a psychological case. Jesus's voice and telepathic command summoned him straight out of his affliction, so he picked up his mat, as he had been told, and walked off. The moment he is rebuked for working on the Sabbath by carrying this mat around – carrying a burden on the Sabbath was work, and carrying this wretched mat was deemed to be carrying a burden – we can be fairly sure that this is an account of something that really happened. Even more convincing is the healed man's saying that he did not know who had told him to pick up his mat in the first place: he had merely done as he had been told by someone with a very authoritative voice. We learn more of Jesus's ways when the witness reports that Jesus later came across the healed man and told him not to sin again in case something worse should happen. This was clearly uttered in jocular fashion, showing that Jesus understood well that this ordinary person intuitively knew that the association of disease with sin was often mistaken.

The fourth sign, which appears in every Gospel, the feeding of the 5,000, must have been so widely established a story that omitting it was not an option. It is unlikely that the writer obtained the number of participants from the witness; he will have quoted that number because it will have been part of the tradition. However, the added details are likely to have come from the witness. We have Jesus asking Philip specifically where food for the crowd might be obtained, although the idea that Jesus asked Philip to test him has to be the writer's interpretation and not information from the witness. Similarly, the singling out of Andrew, Simon Peter's brother, as the one who found the boy with five barley loaves – the cheapest available – and two preserved fish, indicates input from the witness. The crucial detail, which is *not* noted in the other three Gospels, is that this happened at the time of the Passover when travellers would very nearly all have had the small baskets, which almost every Jew carried, with food for 'emergencies' in them. They, being culturally careful and provident, would put into these baskets anything useful they might pick up as they went around. This makes it very possible that the 'miracle' on this occasion was all the people being persuaded to share what they had, one with another, when the wonderful example was set by the generous-minded young lad. A small detail confirms the credibility of the story as it is said that Jesus decided to leave quickly, because the crowd intended to make him king. This is not surprising on their part, as the sort of king who could persuade the rich to share their wealth with the poor was exactly what they all wanted. Following this, the disciples crossed the Sea of Galilee without Jesus and were caught by a sudden storm when they were much closer to land than they realised. They must have thought that they recognised Jesus's shape in the gloom, but imagined it was his ghost, as he seemed to be walking on the water. They were terrified; Jesus had to calm them down.

The next part of the chapter contains precise details which must have come from the witness while there is a considerable amount of teaching which is almost certainly from the writer. The crowd's question, 'Rabbi, when did you get here?' will be from the witness but the 'Truly, truly' tells us that at least much of what follows is from the writer. The 'I say to you, begin working…for the food that keeps into eternal life' is clearly from the writer while the question from the crowd, 'What sign are you going to produce?', giving as an example the manna given to the Jews when they were trekking through the wilderness on their way from Egypt to the Promised Land, will have come from the witness. Jesus then must have said something about true bread from God (Lord's

Prayer, again), but the request from the crowd that Jesus should always give them this bread – they think it is normal bread – must be from the witness. We then have the extraordinary exchanges in which Jesus is reported as saying that they will have to eat his flesh and drink his blood – meant, of course, spiritually, which they did not understand – which was totally contrary to Jewish law and tradition. The witness must have reported something like this but we cannot be sure exactly what. The statement that, as a result of this interchange, many of his disciples gave up following him, must be from the witness and confirmed as true, as it is not what satisfactorily conforms with the image of Jesus's divine status which the writer wants to project. The truth of it all is validated in the last question and answer, when Jesus asks his closest followers if they want to leave him too and Simon Peter, their spokesman, responds with his plaintive question about to whom else should they go, especially as Jesus's words have eternal life in them. This must be from the witness.

Chapter 7 starts with Jesus's brothers urging him to go to the Festival of Tabernacles, which is also called Sukkot and occurs on the fifteenth day of the seventh month. It is obvious that they were hoping that he would be a clear and complete failure and then leave the public scene. The manner of Jesus's dismissal of their suggestion shows he was condemning their attitude. It would seem that the witness was at the festival before

Jesus, because he noticed how the crowd was asking where Jesus might be and how some people were saying Jesus was a good man while others were saying that he was leading the people astray, echoing the account in the Babylonian Talmud which records, as has been said, that one Yeshu (Hebrew for Jesus) was hung (crucified) on the eve of the Passover for sorcery and leading Israel astray. Jesus's telepathic and healing powers were so remarkable that they were thought to amount to what mediaeval people called witchcraft.

The chapter seems to be a mixture of witness and writer. The crowd's thinking that Jesus was paranoid and Jesus's claiming that some people wanted to have him killed must have come from the witness. Similarly, even though we do not know what 'the one amazing deed' is, to which reference is being made, we clearly have input from the witness. Even more likely to be from the witness is the description of the crowds remarking that here is Jesus speaking publicly – again – and no one is doing anything to stop him. Could this be because the authorities had concluded that Jesus's mission was divine after all? The crowd's continuation seems witness based: "However, we actually know where this man comes from; when the Christ appears, no one is going to know where he comes from." Jesus goes on to say that he has not come of his own accord. Later in the chapter we have some people saying, "This really is the prophet," while others said, "This is the Christ." We then have, in effect, the coup de grace when some said, "Is the Christ to come from Galilee? [John has already made it clear that Jesus does]. Has not the scripture said that the Christ is to be a direct descendant of David and from the village of Bethlehem, where David was?" [The writer avoids supporting the idea put forward here]. The final nail in the coffin of the idea that John might *not* have been slightly ambivalent about the messianic role of Jesus is his reproducing, *unqualified*, the statement from the authorities, "Are you from Galilee too? Search and you will find that no prophet is to rise from Galilee," although Jonah was from Galilee, which the writer will have known all too well. The officers had just failed to return with Jesus and Nicodemus had suggested that Jesus should be allowed the right to say something before he was condemned. John has avoided supporting the idea that Jesus was the Messiah, even though he has often written of others suggesting he was. Perhaps he at least half understood that Jesus was far, far more than just a special saviour for the Jews, the Messiah or Christ in Greek, as foretold by the prophets. Jesus's statement that they knew where he had come from must be from the witness as well, confirming that the crowd and Jesus considered his parents to be Joseph and Mary. The wondering about whether Jesus was going to join other Jews living outside Israel (the Diaspora) will have been from the witness, particularly the claim on the part of Jesus that they would not be able to come where he was going and that when they looked for him they would not find him.

An important piece of the witness's input is the sending of officers to arrest Jesus, which was in addition to some of the crowd wanting to have him arrested. The importance of this is made clear when those sent to arrest Jesus return to the High Priest's authorities without Jesus and the witness has run back to find out how they will be greeted after failing to do what they had been told to do. Children, who remember being scolded for failures, like to know what happens to others, particularly to grown-ups, when they have failed, as this time the pain is not being suffered by them. The witness will have been very pleased that the officers said that no one ever before had spoken in the way his idol Jesus did. He will have been impressed when the authorities asked if the officers had been led astray by Jesus, as well as others, who are all categorised as a bunch of ignoramuses. It is very interesting that the witness records that a member of the court, Nicodemus, who had visited Jesus by night to interrogate him, pointed out that someone should not be condemned before his side of the case had been heard. Even more interesting is the question, "You do not come from Galilee too, do you? Do some research and you will find that no prophet comes from Galilee", followed by 'and they all went home'. This is all straight from the witness, the failure to remember that the prophet Jonah came from Galilee being the last straw to break the back of any case that tries to cast doubt on the truth of the story.

The account of the woman caught in adultery, which opens chapter 8, is different in style and choice of some words from the other stories and so, even though it may come from a witness, is unlikely to have come from *our* witness, John, the son of Zebedee, and may have been incorporated into the Gospel by another hand later. Anyway, it sounds rather more like a story with a moral or a fable from Aesop than an account of a real event. An interesting twist to this story is the instruction that he who is without sin is the one who should cast the first stone. In a stoning the ones to cast the first stones were supposed to be the prime witnesses (Deuteronomy 17:7). At that time they were *all without sin* until they could be shown to have transgressed the Law in some identifiable way.

The claim from Jesus that he is the light of the world and that his teaching provides a light for everyone to see the right path through life, followed by the accusation that he is bearing witness to himself, suggests witness input. It is likely that some of the accusers may know of the endorsement of Jesus by John the Baptist; they will certainly know of his deeds of healing, exorcism and telepathic understanding and have witnessed for themselves his knowledge of scripture and law when he had been only a Galilean joiner-builder before. All this witness speaks to something more than some of them might have wanted to believe. The specific allusions to particular quotations from scripture will come from the knowledge of the writer but the fact that scripture was cited is likely to have come from the witness.

When we have Jesus teaching but suddenly have the question put, "Who is your father?" we may be fairly sure that this was triggered by a memory from the witness. The conflict between witness and writer is indicated by the juxtaposition of Jesus saying one moment, "I judge no one" [witness] and then, the very next moment, "While if I do judge, my judgement is true because I am not judging on my own: but I and the one who sent me (judge together)", which is mostly from the writer, although the Gospel's central point, that God is directing Jesus all the time, is implied in this part of the passage.

More witness based dialogue follows, which is heavily interpreted by the writer, repeating the theme of Jesus going away and that they will vainly look for him. Suddenly, we have the question, which must surely come from the witness, "Who (exactly) are you?" which is answered indirectly as Jesus's being, in effect, exactly what he has shown himself to be all the time since his baptism by John the Baptist. He has been acting as God's directed representative on earth all the time. The final description of them knowing what is going on when Jesus is 'lifted up' is likely to be from the writer's perspective. The crucifixion and its comparison with the lifting up of the fiery serpent, which the Lord had commanded Moses to make and elevate so that all who looked on it would be saved from dying of the serpent bites, must be from the writer. Only he will have known well the story from the Book of Numbers, 21:4-9 where God is said to have punished the Israelites for speaking against God and Moses when they were suffering from starvation and thirst after being brought out of Egypt. God had sent serpents that bit them so that many died of the bites and the Israelites had then become repentant. Moses, at their behest, prayed to God for help and, following God's instructions, he made and set up the image of a fiery serpent so that everyone who looked at it would be saved from the bites and live. This was John's parable: 'Look at the image of Jesus on the cross and you will be saved from spiritual death.'

The next part of the chapter continues as a mix of half-remembered material from the witness and the interpretation of the teaching writer. The ideas of slavery and being descended from Abraham almost certainly come from the witness, as the claim that they had never been in slavery is so obviously false to anyone who knows the history, that it is most unlikely to have been invented; they had been slaves to the Egyptians in Egypt, where they might have helped build pyramids, they had been conquered since and now they were under the Romans. However, Jesus's claim that they were slaves to sin (as defined by the Law) is probably correct, once we realise exactly what he is likely actually to have said. The Law under which they were suffering declared that anyone who transgressed any of its nitpicking details was declared by the authorities to be guilty of sin. We saw this when the mat-carrying former paralytic was officially said to be sinning because he was carrying his paltry mat on the Sabbath. This was indeed a form of slavery from which Jesus intended to free everyone. The Law was not complicated, as the 'enslaving' authorities taught, but simple: 'Show your love for God by looking after your neighbour with God in mind and treating everyone with conscious goodwill.' One banishes sin rather more effectively by aiming to do good for individual people than by concentrating on long impersonal lists of intricate commandments so as to avoid doing evil.

We then have a passage that is so intertwined it is very difficult to distinguish what is from the witness and what from the writer. "I know you are descendants of Abraham, but you are still aiming to kill me because my teaching finds no place in your hearts [*this may be part witness and part writer*]. What I have seen when I am alongside my Father is what I am telling you, [*this is the writer interpreting the probable state of affairs in which God is directing Jesus as to what to say*] while you, in like manner, do what you have acquired from your father [*this must be the language of the writer*]." They said

in answer, "Abraham is our father [*witness*]." Jesus said
to them, "If you were Abraham's children, you would do
what Abraham did. But as it is you are aiming to kill
me, a man who has told you the truth (the divine truth)
which I heard from God [*mostly writer, but naming
Abraham and the fact that the source of the truth is God
may come from the witness*]. That is not how Abraham
behaved. You are doing what your father did [*writer*]."
They said "We were not born out of wedlock [*must be
witness*]; we have (only) one father, who is God [*writer
and witness*]." Jesus said to them, "If God were your
father you would love me for it is God from whom I
have come and am now here [*mostly writer as it is Jesus's
teaching that comes straight from God*]. I have not come of
my own accord [*this refers to God's taking over directing
Jesus's life when he was baptised by John and may well be
mostly from the witness*]: it was he (God) who sent me.
Why is it you do not realise what I am talking about?
[*This may be both witness and writer*]. It is because you
cannot take in what I say. You are from your father the
devil and you are set on doing as your father felt inclined
[*perhaps mostly writer*]. He was a murderer from the
beginning [*so strange that it is probably witness based*],
and has nothing of the (divine) truth in his nature
because the truth is not in him [*mostly writer*]. When
he tells a lie he is using his normal language, for he is
a liar and a breeder of lies [*strange enough to be partly
witness based*], while you do not believe me when I am

telling you the (divine) truth. Which of you convicts me of sin? If I tell the truth, why do you not believe me? The one who is from God pays attention to the words of God. The fact that you do not pay attention (to the words of God) shows you are not from God [*writer*]." The crowd of Jews then goes on to say that they think they have put things rather well when they say that Jesus is a Samaritan (or son of the devil) and that he is demented. This must be from the witness. The later statement from Jesus [*writer*], "Your father Abraham was glad to see my day," might be thought of as referring to Abraham's vision of the future but then the writer has Jesus claiming "Before Abraham was I am", 'I Am' being the name the Jews of the time used as the name for God, which must surely be based on some sort of input from the witness as we then have the crowd picking up stones to stone him, which must be from the witness. Jesus was remarkably able, with his way of moving and telepathic powers to influence others, at slipping away as if unobserved, quite possibly with the help of people keen to make sure he was safe.

We then have, in chapter 9, an account that is so graphic that it brings a very real occasion vividly to life before our eyes. This is the fifth sign, the healing of the partially blind man who had been so since birth. Our informant was so amazed at witnessing a blind man being given his sight that every detail was graven indelibly in his memory, particularly the appearance of the man before the authorities. Our witness will have seen many of these inquisitions before, when those subjected to them will have quailed in submission. He will have been amazed at the unprecedented audacity of the now sighted man before these tyrants.

It would seem that the blind man must have been able to see something, although very indistinctly, as he was told to go to a pool and wash his eyes after Jesus had smeared them with mud and spittle. We may deduce this was a state of partial sight, although very limited indeed, as his brain did not seem to have to learn, as our brains do when we are tiny infants, how to interpret the signals from the eyes so that the brain is able to organise the signals into intelligible sensory experiences, for the images that our eyes receive are both upside-down and the wrong way round. However, his disability must have been very acute, as he was clearly considered by himself and everyone else to be 'as good as' blind. Every detail given speaks to a clearly remembered sequence of events. Making the paste, for instance, demonstrates the perceived need for increasing the faith of both patient and those around into believing that he, Jesus, would succeed in giving the man his sight, crowd confidence being a vital part of many apparent miracles. The use of spittle, which was traditionally endowed with special healing qualities, is also very important. The touch of his fingers, when he smeared the eyes of the blind man, would have had healing power too.

The first mark of the authenticity of the occasion is the question as to who was the sinner, the one born blind or the parents; nevertheless, it is clear that part of Jesus's message, which the writer was prominently promoting, was that the law should no longer intrude into every corner of people's lives, while the idea that disease was due to sin was a damaging as well as baseless belief. However, there is a theological theme in the answer, notably the claim that the man had been born blind so that Jesus could provide a sign that God was acting in the world directly through Jesus. All this part is clearly from the writer, who is using the event as a parable to show that with Jesus's aid we, who were in spiritual darkness and so blind, will be able to see with the spiritual touch of Jesus and the light that his teaching provides. The allusion to the fact that Jesus is the light and working in the light only so long as he is in the world, as the coming death of Jesus is the onset of darkness, is obviously from the writer. The reported discussion about whether this was the same man as the one who was born blind is clearly genuine. The chain of events provided by the writer is a marvellous window onto the small world of priestly bureaucratic domination that prevailed at that time. We have some busybodies – the work of healing had been done on the Sabbath – taking the man to the authorities, described as Pharisees. Clearly the witness managed to be at this interrogation as he recounts all the major twists and turns, demonstrating the confusion that Jesus's activities were causing among the powers that were. We have one side saying that working on the Sabbath proved that Jesus was a serious sinner, while the other side, rather more intelligently, points out that 'miraculous' works for good must have their origin in God. First we have the authorities asking the man what he thinks about Jesus his healer, because they want to gauge how much influence he may be having, and he answers that he thinks he must be a prophet, no more, no less. We then have the authorities summoning the parents so as to question them. The parents are very careful to avoid 'incriminating' themselves, so they explain that he is old enough to answer for himself: the authorities should be putting the questions to their son rather than to them. The fact that they question the healed man again is even more compelling, particularly as we have an 'accused' with such a strongly independent mind. The introduction to the second interrogation is begun with words equivalent to swearing an oath to tell the truth. The simplicity of his response, "I cannot say if he is a sinner or not but I can say that I could not see (before he healed me) and now I can", establishes almost irrefutably, complete authenticity for the account. Then we have (which cannot possibly have been invented) the wonderful retort, when he is asked again how he came to be given his sight, "I have told you already; but you did not pay attention [this from the lowest of the low to the highest of the high]. Why do you want to hear it all again? *You do not want to become his disciples too, do you?*" [This is *irrefutably* from a witness to the event.] The vilification visited upon the intended victim by the furious and frustrated accusers is entirely predictable. Their feeble response that they were disciples of Moses and that they did not know where his healer came from gives the victory to the victim when he says, "This is the remarkable bit: you do not know where he comes from yet he is the one who opened my eyes. We know that God does not listen to sinners [actually he does, else we would all be irremediably in trouble] but if someone is god-fearing and does as God wishes, God listens to him. Never throughout the ages has it been heard that someone gave sight to someone born blind. If this man were not from God he would not be able to do anything." They showed they had lost the argument when they replied, just as all dictators do, "You were born in utter sin, yet you are teaching us." And they threw him out (banning him from the synagogue). The whole episode is absolutely riveting and quite unarguably authentic.

The ending is happy when Jesus, discovering the man has been banned from the synagogue, shows he, Jesus, is acting for God in this world and welcomes him into the new way of looking for God.

The interchange about giving sight to the blind and making the sighted blind, although there is likely to be something there from the witness, sounds like the writer remembering similar words in Isaiah. The bit when the Pharisees ask whether they are blind will be from the witness, while the response will have been fashioned mostly by the writer. This chapter is essential reading for everyone, who can read, in the world.

Chapter 10 begins with preaching, although it is very useful to know how shepherds actually looked after their sheep at night and led them out for the day. The idea attributed to Jesus that he had other flocks to attend to is clearly from the writer who lived in the new world in which Judaism was for the Gentiles as well as for the Jews. Even more clearly from the writer comes the claim that Jesus is in complete charge of his destiny, when it was the political and religious authorities who would condemn him and carry out the sentence. However, the moment we hear statements that Jesus is out of his mind, we discern the witness, as this is at variance with the mental set of the writer. The evidence adduced to disprove the accusation of madness, that such a man would not be able to give sight to the blind, is the seal of truth: it all happened just as the record declares.

The seven day festival of dedication, Hanukkah, which may also be called the Festival of Lights, celebrates the dedication of the Second Temple under the Maccabees. It may sometimes, very appropriately, begin on Christmas Eve. The picture of people encircling Jesus at this time and asking him if he is the

Messiah rings true, even if they were actually asking him if he were some great prophet rather than the Messiah. It would seem that Jesus had said something about them not believing his message and did indeed make some claim about his affinity to God as his son. This incited the crowd to pick up stones to stone Jesus. The effect of Jesus's voice is shown to be remarkably powerful: they are stopped in their tracks by it *and* by his amazing unflinching courage, especially his steely confidence. He asks which of his good deeds is a cause for stoning him when they are just about to stone him for making himself equal with God. It seems he had said he was God's son. He astounds them yet again by knowing which of the Psalms speaks of all Israelites being the sons of God. The mixture of writer and witness continues with Jesus pointing out that the proof of the pudding, that would give them the faith in Jesus's message, which they need, is to be found in his deeds of healing. Again, when they try to seize him, he somehow just disappears, presumably with the helping hands of his devoted supporters.

The sixth sign, in chapter 11, is probably the most significant, apart from the crucifixion and Jesus's reappearance after his death. It was even more significant than the giving of sight to the man blind since birth. That had been bad enough for the authorities, but this would seem to have been the last straw; they had to be rid of Jesus as soon as possible. His miraculous deeds were becoming ever more remarkable and increasingly widely known.

Jesus's special friend, Lazarus, had fallen ill and then, a day or two later, into a coma, apparently dead. The writer was certain that Lazarus had died, although the input of the witness makes it clear that he was 'asleep', i.e. in a coma. Jesus's telepathic information gave him to understand that he should not go for a day or two, even though his special friends, the family of Lazarus, were desperate that he should come at once. A telling piece of evidence which backs up the truth of the account is Thomas's exclaiming that they should all go with Jesus to die with him. Jesus had just said that he was going back to where they were going to stone him only a few days before. When Jesus did eventually arrive, the supposedly dead Lazarus was ready to be summoned out of his four day coma. Strong evidence that Lazarus had not been dead is that his body had not decayed. The argument that God had intervened to restore a decayed body is as unnecessary as it is unlikely. God's interventions are likely to be far more subtle than that.

The considerable band of mourners was dumbfounded by Jesus's bringing Lazarus back to life. It is not at all surprising that reports of the miracle spread very fast and far. Enthusiastic crowds wanted to see Jesus, as he was now the equivalent of the very highest royalty. He was, locally, far more famous than anyone in today's tinsel parades of celebrities. The amount of persuasive circumstantial detail provided in the account more or less sets the seal of authenticity on the story, which is further confirmed by the reaction of the authorities: it was a genuine reason for them to feel that the elimination of Jesus was urgent. It is clear that the witness had information from the High Priest's council, else the writer would not have received the information that there had been panic among the members of the High Priest's council and that it was Caiaphas who had sorted out the problem by declaring that it was Jesus alone who should die to save the situation. Jesus's informant, as well as his telepathic powers, will have persuaded him to go to an out-of-the way place after the raising of Lazarus.

With chapter 12 the 'countdown' to the Passover starts. The first event is dinner at the house of Lazarus, where Mary anoints the feet of Jesus with an extremely costly ointment and then wipes them with her hair. The extravagant 'waste' is complained about by Judas Iscariot, who had charge of the common purse. We can tell this comes from the witness as he says, probably with distorting hindsight, that Judas helped himself to its contents on a regular basis. The other disciples would have been likely to notice, had this been the case, and would probably have put a stop to it; Jesus, with his telepathic power, would have noticed too. The event is covered by Mark, who says it was in the house of Simon the Leper in Bethany, and that some complained at the waste. He said Judas then went to the chief priests to propose betraying Jesus. Matthew includes this story, defining the complainers as disciples, before Judas goes to the chief priests. Luke writes of Jesus visiting Mary and Martha in a village close to Jerusalem at this time, but says nothing about the ointment episode happening here. Instead, he places it much earlier (chapter 7) during the ministry, this time in the house of a *Pharisee*, also named Simon, but who was not described as a leper. The lady seems not to have been a guest or named in these other accounts. Luke, in his account, which is as lovely as usual, explains that she is a sinner; he does have the principal details right, in that she anoints his feet, rather than head; otherwise his version bears the hallmarks of an interesting piece that Luke wants to fit in somewhere, without actually knowing anything about its provenance. These other accounts contain fewer details: they are more vague. They are clearly secondhand, while John's description of the smell of the ointment filling the whole house smacks of a vivid memory of the original event. However, it is a convenient metaphor for the writer, as the house may be thought of as the world and the smell of the ointment as Jesus's teaching filling it: Jesus was teaching a new form of Judaism for the whole world, just as Isaiah had foretold. The fact that it was the feet that were anointed adds preferability to the Johannine account, as anointing the head would be ascribing honour to the anointer as well as to the anointed.

Then we have the event we celebrate as Palm Sunday. It will have been the fame won by Jesus when he resuscitated Lazarus that will have attracted the crowds to Jerusalem on this day. Only such an event as raising the dead could persuasively be advanced as an attraction sufficient to draw such crowds. The crowd attraction, because of Lazarus, both confirms the raising of Lazarus as true and explains the High Priest's decision to try to have Lazarus eliminated as well as Jesus. The description of people in the crowds carrying bundles of palm, myrtle and willow, although not associated with Passover, is given in all the Gospels, so it is difficult to dismiss. It would seem likely that a member of the crowd decided, on a sudden impulse, to fling his bundle into the path of Jesus as he was coming on the ass and many others copied, as people in crowds so often do. The information that a report of this large concourse welcoming Jesus caused further consternation among the authorities might be writer calculation or might actually have come from the witness.

An authenticating detail is that some Greeks wanted to meet Jesus and that they asked Philip to help; even stronger validation is given when Philip goes on to tell Andrew, Simon Peter's brother, about this and they go to Jesus together. The writer does not tell us what transpired; instead, he provides prophesying from Jesus. The writer has Jesus making prophecies about his coming glorification, which is the antithesis of the idea of crucifixion. This is most unlikely to be from the witness.

What Jesus was actually saying at the critical moment we are not in a position to calculate but there is likely to have been a sudden thunderclap, as such information is more likely to have come from the witness than the imagination of the writer. However, we are sharply lifted out of the world of make-believe into the realms of reality with the crowd's response to the sayings attributed to Jesus by the writer. Jesus was reported as having said, "Now is the moment of judgement for this world; now shall the ruler of this world be thrown out. And I, if I am lifted up from the earth, will draw everyone to myself." The crowd suddenly asked, "We have been taught from the law that the Christ stays for ever so how do you come to say that the Son of man must be lifted up? [*this part is likely to be witness and writer*] Who is this son of man, anyway [*this is from the witness*]?" The writer then takes over again with an answer that does not fit the question at all. Then there is another of the apparently frequent disappearing acts, when Jesus slips away with his manner of moving and help from his supporters.

At the last supper, in chapter 13, we start with some theological setting of the scene by the writer before we have the celebrated washing of the disciples' feet by Jesus. This event is not chronicled in the other Gospels. Luke, however, says that there had been a dispute as to which of them should be the greatest. Jesus provides an answer here, as washing feet was a task for the lowest ranked servant in a house; Jesus was, in effect, telling his disciples that even the most menial servant is as important as the master, while the greatest disciple is the one who provides the greatest service. The detail that confirms that this really happened is the interchange between Simon Peter and Jesus: "You Lord, do you wash my feet [*one may almost feel the uncomprehending incredulity*]?" Jesus said in answer, "You do not yet understand what I am doing at this very moment, but you will, after these things." Peter said, "You shall never ever wash my feet!" Jesus answered him, "If I do not wash you, you have no part with me." Simon Peter said, "Then, Master, not my feet only, but my hands and head too!" None of this can possibly be novelistic invention: it is a completely faithful snapshot of an event in an otherwise inaccessible past. Jesus said to him, "Anyone who has bathed [possibly in public baths before coming to the meal] does not need to wash, apart from his feet, as he is then clean all over." It may be clear that after bathing only the feet will be dirtied by walking, but otherwise the explanation provided by the writer does not quite fit with what Jesus has been demonstrating to them. Suddenly, we have the declaration from Jesus that one of them is going to betray him. Clearly this happened, and Jesus's telepathic understanding will have alerted him as to who was going to do it and when.

The certainly authentic communication between Peter and the witness disciple about the identity of the traitor will not have been noticed by anyone else at the supper. However, the dipping and giving of a morsel was associated with a Passover meal rather than any other; perhaps this was felt to be the equivalent to a Passover meal as Jesus was to be crucified just before. One imagines that the witness learned about what the other disciples thought from what he heard them muttering as they saw Judas leaving. It might have taken this form: 'Where's Judas off to now?' 'I don't know; perhaps he is going to make arrangements for something.'

There follows some preaching which contains a statement that is almost certain to be based on input from the witness: "Children, I am with you for a little longer; you will look for me, and, just as I told the Jews that where I am going you cannot go, so I am telling you this now. **A new commandment I give you, that you love one another, just as I have loved you (especially) so that you also would come to love one another. By *this* everyone will know that you are my disciples, *just so long as you love one another.*"**

This passage is the core of Jesus's teaching. It is then followed by a passage, the first part of which is almost guaranteed to be virtually an exact record: Simon Peter said to him, "*Master, where are you going?*" Jesus answered, "*I am going where you cannot follow me at the moment*, but later on you will follow." Peter said, "*Lord, why cannot I follow you now? I will lay down my life for you*." Jesus answered, "Will you really lay down your life for me [he did]? Truly, truly, I say to you, *cock-crow will definitely not sound until you have denied me three times*." The record of events more or less guarantees all this except that part which forms the statement that Peter will follow later, implying that he will suffer the same death. This is more likely to have been added by the writer, to demonstrate Jesus's prescience. Perhaps, '*although you may follow later*' could be more likely.

We then continue with the often repeated themes that Jesus is to be with them for only a short time more and that they should love one another, with the strange statement, "In my father's house there are many dwelling places [not the 144,000, derived from Revelation 7:4, for which the sealed redeemed were to be selected specifically only from the tribes of Israel: the Jehovah's Witnesses may not have understood properly the basis of their belief]. I am going so as to prepare a place for you." It is in *this* world that change may be expected, not, one would think, in the *eternal* one beyond ours, whatever it may be. This suggests that the witness has said something vaguely similar but that the writer has misunderstood. We then have the theme of Jesus coming back, which is very likely to be based on witness statements. Similarly, we may have some confidence in the idea that there will be communication with us, and strengthening comfort for us, from God via the Holy Spirit.

A validating passage is provided by Thomas when, Jesus having said, apparently, "I shall come again and take you to myself, so that where I am you may also be and *to where I am going you know the way*," Thomas says, "Master, we do not know where you are going; how are we to know the way?" Jesus replies, "I am the way, the (divine and real) truth and the life; no one comes to the Father except through me. If you had come to know who I was, you would know my Father also. From now on you do know him and have seen him." Philip provided further confirmation with his "Master, show us the Father, and that will be enough for us." Jesus said to him, "Have I been with you for so long, Philip, and you still have not come to know me? Anyone who has seen me has (in effect) seen the Father." This is all far too realistic to have been invented; it must be witness-based but heavily shaped by the thinking of the writer. It is the teaching of Jesus that shows the way but actually 'seeing' something which is in the totally different next world cannot be on any human agenda. This makes it clear that the writer does not always understand the information he has been given.

There follows much preaching but also another multiple nugget when Judas who is not 'Iscariot' asks, "Master, how has it come about that you are destined to *reveal* yourself to us and *not to the world*?" It is clear, both from the unexpected identification of the questioner and from the very extended answer attributed to Jesus, that this question was indeed posed, but without the writer fully appreciating its significance. Jesus is indeed destined to come back, but in a form that is recognised only by the favoured few followers of Jesus – and even then they sometimes needed extra clues to know that it was Jesus whom they were seeing. All the details and the slight inaccuracy establish the authenticity. The slight inaccuracy was that Jesus also appeared – or was revealed – to his sceptical brother James, who had not believed in him, and as an unseen but electrifying experience to Saul, very much an unbeliever, on the road to Damascus.

—

FIVE

THE TRIAL OF JESUS AND
THE FINAL DOUBLE SIGN

This chapter starts with one of the most significant pieces of information anywhere in this part of the story, so long as the commentators are right in saying that the Kedron, which they crossed after the supper to reach the garden, flowed with water only when there was a considerable fall of rain. One would not expect such weather at the time of the Passover, yet our witness, according to the Greek text, said it was a torrent. Something was flowing in such quantities that this often dry water course was described as being in full flow, *a torrent*. If it had not rained, this full flow can be accounted for only if it was the blood of the lambs that had been slaughtered in preparation for the Passover, since the wadi served as a drain from the Temple. The number of lambs slaughtered could have been two hundred thousand, or even more, explaining the otherwise inexplicably torrential state of the wadi. Provided this information is right, we are safe in believing that John's timing of the Last Supper is also right: it was the night before Passover, not the Passover meal itself.

When the band of Temple officers arrived to arrest Jesus we are told by the witness that Jesus actually stepped forward himself and asked them whom they were looking for. When they said 'Jesus of Nazareth' he then said 'I am he' in such a way that they all fell to the ground. Clearly they were taken completely by surprise that he was so unafraid that he acknowledged at once who he was, but that would not seem enough make them all fall to the ground. One may suspect that Jesus may have made the declaration in a surprisingly unusual voice, perhaps as if it were from someone from beyond the grave. His sense of humour almost certainly never deserted him unless he were confronted by intolerable injustice. Jesus had to repeat the question and once more said he was the one they were looking for, with the added plea that they allow his other followers to go free. This time they arrested him and him alone. We then have the quite unexpected and most inexpert assault by

Peter on the High Priest's agent. Mark's Gospel relates this, and, if this report is, as surmised, based on what Peter said when he was spreading the message of Jesus, we have very good further evidence to support the truth of the account. That the assailant was unnamed in Mark is what one would expect, as Peter would not have risked incriminating himself and he might not have wanted other people to know how incompetent he had been with a sword. We are then told that the first part of the 'trial' was in the house of Annas, where the witness is unlikely to have had easy access, and then in the house of the High Priest where nothing is reported as having happened. The other Gospels do not include the house of Annas in Jesus's itinerary. The report of what happened describes a scene that belonged to a totally different era, thus increasing the strength of the evidence that the Gospel depended on detailed and accurate eye-witness material. The writer reminds us that it was Caiaphas who was the High Priest that year and that it was he who had proposed that one man should die to save the status quo.

Next comes a remarkably detailed account of how Peter gained admission to the High Priest's house. We have Peter staying outside until the witness disciple asks a servant girl, who is described as on duty at the door and as knowing this disciple, to let Peter in. The accuracy of the record is highlighted by the almost immediate suggestion from the girl that Peter must be a follower of Jesus too, as she will certainly have known that the witnessing disciple was a follower, while the deduction on her part that the connection between the two was Jesus, is thus explained. The witness will have heard every denial made by Peter although it would seem that he could not identify the second questioner. It should be emphasised that these denials could not be described, by any stretch of the imagination, as cowardly: they were absolutely essential if Peter was to have a chance of surviving long enough to spread Jesus's message. The details that they were warming themselves by a charcoal fire and that the third questioner was a relation of Malchus, coming from a truth-dedicated writer, are such strong evidence for eye-witness input that the case for dual authorship becomes almost irrefutable. Then we have the sounding of the cockcrow signal (possibly double). Mark's Gospel, which is probably based on information obtained from Peter himself via John Mark, coupled with the record of the witness, guarantees the truth of this famous story. It is almost as inescapably true as the fact that Jesus was crucified: any person who denies that Jesus was crucified is as wilfully blind as those who deny that the Nazis mass-murdered Jews and so puts very seriously into question the reliability of any other statement such a person might choose to make.

We now have the questioning of Jesus by the High Priest, which amounts, almost, to an attempt to entice the 'accused' into self-incrimination and so is totally contrary to correct practice. One suspects that proper procedure should require first an accusation then a chance for presenting a case for defence. Therefore, the report that the proceedings began with a question about what Jesus had been teaching, rather than stating an accusation, indicates that the proceedings were being conducted irregularly and that this account is also a correct record of events, as conjuring up such a chain of events is neither in the writer's armoury nor in his character. Even more powerful evidence of both truth and impropriety is provided by the interchange when Jesus points out correctly that the question should be asked of those who had heard his teaching and not of him. This is followed by an attending official striking Jesus because he had gauged from the tone of Jesus's response that he was correcting the High Priest. This officer clearly did not know what the correct procedure was. It was not normal for the accused not only to know his rights but also to demand that they be respected, hence, probably, the unjustified behaviour on the part of the officer. Even stronger evidence is provided by the continuation of the account when Jesus says that the officer should produce the evidence for his decision to strike Jesus or, in effect, apologise, when Jesus continues with, "(then) why strike me?" This will not have been invented: it happened more or less just as the witness has said.

The continuation of the story saying that Jesus was sent bound to the house of the High Priest, where it is quite clear that he has just been questioned, demonstrates the relationship between writer and witness and the way of proceeding. The witness, being unable to read, was not in a position to correct errors, while the dissimilarity between writer and witness meant that there was no adequate mental rapport between the two that might have enabled them to realise when mistakes were being made, even though each was absolutely sure of the overwhelming importance of Jesus. Their devotion to Jesus had totally different bases: the witness's was from personal knowledge and unbridled adoration, while the writer's was based on what he had read and heard without ever actually meeting Jesus. The writer, though clearly a Jew, was probably a member of the Diaspora, possibly even before Jesus began his ministry.

When Jesus has been led next to the praetorium in the very early morning, we are told that the Jews remained outside so as not to be defiled – rendered unclean through being in a non-Jewish dwelling place. This detail is not to be expected from one devoted to the truth if it is not fact, so we should accept that this is further evidence that this all happened on the day before Passover. The other Gospels do not give proper details of the interchange between Jesus and Pilate except the question, 'Are you king of the Jews?' to which

Jesus, in them, assents without further explanation – 'You have said so' would be better translated as 'As you say.' The account in John has real provenance, for here his kingdom is clearly stated to be not of this world and so no challenge whatsoever to the territorial claims to sovereignty on the part of Caesar (Tiberius), the second Roman Emperor.

An interesting detail, not found in the other Gospels, is Pilate's telling the Jews to deal with the problem themselves and their reply that only the Romans have the right to put anyone to death. Before this we have wonderful detail. Pilate asks what is their accusation and the reply, when a writer of fiction of that time would have given the actual accusation, prevaricates: "If the man had not done wrong, we would not have brought him before you." The other Gospels give a clear accusation in that Jesus claimed, they alleged, that he was King. No such clarity is found here, which is much more true to life. Pilate's elliptical reply – they have not said what Jesus is guilty of – is that they should judge him themselves then. This, also, is completely true to life.

Then we have the complete confirmation that this actually happens as described: Pilate, with condescending mockery, one suspects, says, "So you are king of the Jews are you?" with Jesus asking, instead of giving the appropriate answer, "Was it your idea to ask this or did others hand in a report about me?". The writer is totally incapable of having concocted this, not just because he is devoted to truth but because he just does not have the brilliant psychological understanding demonstrated here: this all has to have happened almost exactly as described. Even more decisive evidence for authenticity is provided when the interchange continues with Pilate indignantly spitting out, "I am not a Jew, am I? Your own people and the chief priests [it was only the chief priests] have handed you over to me. What (on earth) have you done?" The claim to kingship is left out at this point, so Jesus's reply is again elliptical, "My kingdom is not of this world." Anyone who believes that all this could possibly have been invented has not engaged in effective thinking. The suggestion that Jesus's supporters would have fought to save him is also interesting: Peter had tried and had made a complete hash of it; the others would probably have been even more useless, but they had already run away. Jesus continues with his claim to be a king (when Pilate actually puts the question), but not of this world, and that he came into the world to bear witness to the divine truth. We then have a most remarkable query from Pilate, for which the answer is not given; Pilate may not have waited for it as the legend has it: "What is truth?". Plenty of philosophers profess to be confused by this question nowadays. This simple-minded writer thinks that 'Jesus' should be the answer: he is the truth! Next comes the part of the story outlined in all the Gospels: should Pilate release

Barabbas or Jesus? But the crowd has been well selected and primed. The bandit is the one who is chosen for release.

The 'trial' conducted by Pilate seems to start with Pilate thinking that Jesus was deluded but ends with him realising that he had never met anyone like this before. He will have been amazed by the calm and rational demeanour of one who faced such an excruciating penalty; he is most unlikely to have been confronted with such composure before in one who was being threatened with so terrifying a death.

The scourging of Jesus, although the only reason for it is tradition, is attested by all the Gospels, and so will have occurred. Pilate may have felt frustrated by the actual course of events and so 'taken this out' on Jesus, who was otherwise completely innocent as far as Roman law was concerned.

The crown of thorns, although it might be one of acanthus, comes in Mark and Matthew as well as John, but not in Luke. The purple robe (scarlet in Luke) is also well attested. 'Behold the man!' is unique to John, as is much else; for instance, Pilate tells the 'Jews' to crucify Jesus themselves, to which the Jews answered, "We have a law and according to the law he ought to die as he has set himself up as the son of God." We then have further powerful evidence that all has actually been witnessed when Pilate is described as being dismayed – he was probably very irritated – and then asked Jesus where he was from. It is quite inconceivable that this was invented. This is followed by another completely genuine memory of the occasion: Jesus did not reply and Pilate then asked, "Will you not speak to me? Surely you know that I have authority to release you and authority to crucify you?"This may be another coup de grace when Jesus says, although it is in line with the thinking of the writer, "You would have no authority over me if it had not been granted you from above, so the one who handed me over to you is guilty of the greater sin."

Inescapably from a witness again is the interchange between Pilate and the assembled concourse when Pilate, apparently keen to release Jesus, is confronted with "If you set this man free you are not a friend of Caesar's; anyone who sets himself up as king is making a claim against Caesar." We then, uniquely, have the account of Pilate bringing Jesus out of the praetorium and his taking up a position sitting on a raised step known as Gabbatha in Hebrew. This extra detail is not in the other Gospels and it is not in the character of the writer to invent all this: it will have happened more or less exactly as related here. The scene is further enhanced with its being about noon on the day of preparation (for Passover?) and Pilate asking, "Shall, I crucify your king?" This will probably have been uttered in tones of mockery. The answer from the chief priests, "We have no king but Caesar", was a total denial of what they were supposed to claim for the incorrigibly independent Jews. This is all ineluctably genuine.

There is general agreement that the site of crucifixion was called the Place of the Skull (Golgotha), that Jesus carried the crossbeam of his cross himself, until one named Simon of Cyrene might have been recruited to carry it instead, that three were crucified and that Jesus's clothes were divided among the soldiers. Only John details four soldiers, that the clothes were divided into four parts and that lots were cast for a seamless garment, even though this last detail might just have been added to fulfil a scripture. That the superscription, 'Jesus of Nazareth the King of the Jews', was written in Hebrew, Latin and Greek is again unique to John. The other Gospels wrote of the superscription as declaring only that Jesus was the King of the Jews; they seemed keen to distance Jesus from his Nazareth connections. Also unique is the demand from the High Priest's brigade that the inscription be preceded by the statement that Jesus *said* he was king, and that Pilate replied, "What I have written, I have written." These words are deeply engraved in the annals of time. Only the witnessing disciple, out of all Jesus's male followers, was there and only he could have provided such remarkable detail. We then have the extraordinary consignment of Jesus's mother, Mary, to be the witness's mother. Not only does this confirm the veracity of the whole account but demonstrates that this comes straight from the witness responsible for everything that has been recorded as having happened. From then on, we may assume, she lived with the Zebedee family and the witness disciple may have learnt much from her, even if we do not know what. We have other witnesses detailed as Mary Magdalene and Mary, wife of Clopas. This Clopas may have been the 'Cleopas' who features in Luke's beautiful account of Jesus joining the two journeying to Emmaus.

There is no agreement as to what Jesus actually said when he was on the cross, while the assigning of Mary to the witness disciple as his mother will have been so overwhelming a memory that it would have almost obliterated everything else. However, Jesus almost certainly said, "My God, my God, why hast thou forsaken me?", which the writer very predictably does not record and "I thirst", so that we have the offering of vinegar soaked in a sponge at the end of a strip of hyssop, in John as an analgesic and in Luke, where it is not asked for, as an insult. The choice of the Greek word by the writer, which is translated as 'It is finished', suggests triumphant completion, which, although arguably apposite, may have come more from the imagination of the writer than actual reality.

This time the repetition of the statement that it was the day of preparation, particularly when one remembers that, for Jews, crucified bodies were not supposed to stay 'up' for more than the day anyway and certainly not on the Sabbath, invites one to wonder if the day has not been 'adjusted' by the writer after all – but the evidence of the wadi Kedron being in spate could put an end to that. Mark 15: 42 and Luke 23:54 also say it was the day of preparation. Mark says that a centurion certified that Jesus was dead. Only John has the breaking of the legs of the other two victims and the piercing of Jesus's side, with blood and water flowing out from the wound, and only John mentions Nicodemus as collaborating with Joseph of Arimathea to take the body away to 'burial' in a new and unused tomb nearby. Matthew says that the tomb, actually belonging to the rich man, Joseph, had been hollowed out of the rock by him.

Particularly revealing is the statement in 19:35, 'And he who saw this has borne witness and his witness is true [the writer was convinced by what he had heard from the witness] and that man knows that he speaks the truth so that you too may believe.' Here the '**that** man' emphasises that the witness is someone else other than the writer, while the 'we' indicates a group present at this moment, when he is writing down this powerful point, joining in with this emphatic flourish.

Luke has unspecified women, who had come from Galilee, as visiting the tomb on the Sunday, while Mark has three women visiting the tomb on the Sunday: Mary, mother of Jesus, Mary Magdalene and Salome, who may be both the mother of John the witness and the sister of Jesus's mother. As John's aunt, Mary, as has been pointed out already, would be an ideal new 'mother' for the youth. Mark appears to say no more, as there seems to be no reliable extant ending to his Gospel. But in John we have only Mary Magdalene visiting the tomb and she specifically informs just Peter and the witnessing disciple; this is the account we may more safely trust. A revealing point is raised by the fact that Peter and the witness are together; they were by now, it might seem, more often together during daylight hours than apart. The added description of its being comparatively dark at the time, increases the likelihood of this account being totally trustworthy.

We now have an account that is inconceivable without the witness being someone actually involved. Peter and he ran to the tomb, the witness outrunning Peter, but, having looked inside, he waited for Peter before going into the tomb himself. When he did, he found the burial cloths lying as if they had hardly been disturbed. The final 'proof' is that the napkin that had been round the head of the corpse was rolled up in a place by itself. An imagination even more fertile than that of Luke would have to be attributed to the writer if this detail could have been conjured up by him. Even more remarkable is the statement that the grave cloths were still there. This will not have been invention, so a 'normal' removal of the body by someone or other cannot be accepted as a satisfactory explanation for the disappearance of the body: they would not have have gone to the lengths of carefully unwrapping the body and then arranging the winding cloths so that they would appear to have been relatively undisturbed, before taking the corpse away.

What exactly the two disciples believed is not precisely specified, except that they still had some sort of trust in Jesus, even though he was supposed to be dead, nor does the scripture of Jesus rising from the dead seem to be sourced. They were said not to know it yet anyway.

The account of Mary seeing two angels is most unlikely to be witness based and might have been some sort of hallucination. Her thinking that she was talking to the gardener, when she had turned from the tomb, demonstrates most clearly that Jesus was now very different from what he had been in his previous life; even his voice, which must have been far more distinctive than most, was unrecognised. It is ridiculous to suggest that this might have been fabricated: it does not even project the image of a solid body that the Gospel writers wanted to project. Another important indicator of exactly how the resurrection was happening is the instruction to Mary Magdalene from the resurrected Jesus, "Do not touch me!" It is clear that the witness had told the writer that Jesus had said this but the witness will not have given any explanation. Like Peter during the transfiguration, the writer felt he had to provide an explanation, but had no idea what, so he came up with "because I am not yet ascended to the Father". This cannot be thought to be a satisfactory reason as there is no logic in it. Therefore, it is worth trying to work out a reason. This seems relatively easy: Jesus may have been there very convincingly in her mind's eye, even though she had not recognised him properly, but he would *not* be felt by her touch if she tried to hug him. He did not want to frighten Mary as he was not very different from a ghost. Jesus may have told Thomas to touch him a few verses later, but then he knew that Thomas would not do so *or* that Thomas would imagine he was touching something when he was not actually doing so. Anyway, the sight of the resurrected Jesus was probably enough to convince Thomas that Jesus was indeed back in some form.

It might be worth remembering that anyone who disbelieves in ghosts, merely because that person has not experienced them personally, is being obtusely arrogant. In exactly the same way anyone who disbelieves in the *possibility* of there being a God in general, and in the *possibility* of the resurrection experiences in particular, is also being obtusely arrogant. The resurrection accounts, being attested from a number of different sources, are as good as proved by the quantity – might I add 'and quality'? – of independent witness to their having actually happened. The fact that any one person is not capable of believing something personally is no indication that *that* person can logically be so sure that others are wrong in their beliefs, that he (or she) may say categorically that the believers are wrong: this is foolhardy, while refusal dispassionately to assess the evidence, when the matter may be of supreme importance, is being rashly bigoted.

Now we have the strange account of Jesus's first appearance to a meeting of disciples on the day following the Sabbath. It starts with details that are unlikely to have been invented, as well as an omission of why they should be gathered in the first place and, more important, what they were discussing. We may only guess that they were trying to work out what their next steps should be and that they were in some fear of the authorities as they had bolted the doors. Jesus, though disembodied, shows psychological grasp of what is needed to bolster their spirits. He shows his hands and his sides. Jesus is then said to have breathed on them to impart the Holy Breath of God. How much detail is from the writer and how much from the witness is hard to work out here. All we may be fairly sure of is that there was a meeting and that Jesus appeared at it. However, we may be sure that the idea that Jesus was giving them the power of *remitting* sins comes from the writer. We are not told how Jesus disappeared from sight. But we are told that Thomas was not there, which will not be invention. Neither will be the statement to the effect from Thomas that he would not believe until he actually saw Jesus himself, and proof – the wounds suffered from crucifixion – that it was really Jesus there before him. When Jesus appeared at the next meeting at which Thomas was present, he will have known that Thomas would not actually touch him or that if he did, psychological imagination would persuade him that he was touching something that was not actually there. However, the subsequent sayings attributed to Jesus may have come rather more from the writer than the witness.

The writer ends the chapter, clearly thinking that his task is done: Jesus had done many other things which his disciples had witnessed, but he had chosen these seven specially to prove to his readers that Jesus had come from God and that they should believe in him and his teaching.

It is probable that the witness had told the writer before about the remarkable fishing expedition but that the writer had felt he had written enough without mentioning this. It contained no new facets of what Jesus had been teaching and seemed redundant to his purposes, if not even unhelpful as a distraction. However, he seems to have woken up to the fact that he had not really provided quite enough evidence to establish beyond doubt in the minds of his desired readers that the source of his information was impeccable. He will have realised too, that the disciples had not started their mission when they were supposed to do so. He felt he should 'explain' what really 'got them going' and demonstrate more clearly the quality and character of the source of his material. To prove that this added chapter really belonged to the rest of the Gospel he tried to make verses 1-23 of the chapter 496 words long, so as to correspond with the

496 syllables of the prologue (vv. 1-18) to the Gospel in chapter 1. The writer might even have put in at the end of the list of personnel, as an afterthought, the extra seven words saying that there were two other disciples, so as to arrive at the desired number of 496. Arriving at this number precisely depends on which text one uses.

There are general points that stand out in this coda. It is almost entirely without any preaching or exegesis, it starts with carefully arranged and possibly unprecedented detail as to the setting and how everything occurred, and then it specifically names, in a way that is not done anywhere else in the Gospel, precisely the personnel involved, except for two unnamed disciples. Another feature, the only time in this Gospel, is the *naming* of Zebedee and the inclusion of *his* sons, who might, in fact, have been the two unnamed disciples. Even though John's brother James was long dead, mentioning his name might have been considered as endangering his surviving brother, the witness. Five men in a Galilee fishing boat might have been enough anyway. The careful naming of Zebedee, who may not have been a favourite with the writer, because his wealth may have derived from the High Priest's entourage, shows very clearly the writer's determination to lock qualities of credibility, indeed unquestionable reliability, in the derivation of his information, into the record.

It is more or less clear that the disciples felt at a loose end, with nothing particular, let alone anything urgent, to do. They were not getting on with the task with which Jesus had entrusted them.

We do not know if the expedition's failure to catch any fish was 'arranged' by God nor if the charcoal fire had been prepared by someone else with fish already on it. It is quite possible that someone had indeed prepared to have something to eat and gone off for some reason – frightened by an apparition? However, when they are asked from the shore if they have caught any fish, none of them recognises Jesus's voice and certainly not his appearance, as the dawn light was still fairly feeble. On the other hand they do hear the question, which they answer, and they know that a shore based person can just see, because of the way the light slants through the water, where the fish are, when they cannot see this for themselves from their positions in the boat. It is when, having followed the instructions, the catch is so unexpectedly great that Jesus's most devoted follower, and only he, recognises who it is. Attention is instantly drawn to the fact that Peter at once trusts the intuition of the witness and impetuously flings himself into the water to greet Jesus. This is all far too accurately true to character to have been invented. Another detail which nails authenticity into the account is the description of Peter putting on extra clothing before he leapt into the sea: a loin cloth was not sufficient for greeting someone in Jewish culture, which observed religious etiquette all the time. The writer will have known of Luke's account of this trip and was making it clear that this was the correct account because he has competent fishermen hauling the unusually large catch alongside the boat, so as not to run the risk of sinking the boat, and in only one net.

We are not told how the meal went but we then have the most important story in the Gospel, the last evidential details to convince everyone, except the most wilful unbelievers, of the truth of everything that we have been told before. With perfect psychological insight Jesus makes Peter say three times, publicly before the others there, that he loves Jesus, while he is reminded of his three times denial, essential though that had been. To prove he truly loves Jesus he has to start spreading Jesus's message, which he was supposed to have started doing before. Jesus foresees a terrible death for Peter, although we cannot know how much detail was actually outlined by the witness and how much came from the imagination of the writer.

The final nail in the coffin of any possible remaining doubt is the remarkable interchange between Peter and Jesus. Peter happened to turn round, just as Jesus stopped speaking, and saw the witness. His plaintive query, uttered perhaps with a tinge of envious jealousy, "And what is going to happen to this one?", was answered – no imaginative contortions could conceivably have invented this – "If I want him to stay alive until I come, what is that to do with you?" This causes a rumour to go round that the witness is not going to die. The writer and witness are careful to explain exactly what was *not* implied in this response. We then have the final certificate of authenticity: this is the disciple who provided the witness and he and the writer (the Greek text says 'we') know that his witness, is true. A truly revealing postscript is the naive claim from the witness, who had spent so much of his time following Jesus around during those two years or so, that Jesus had done so much that if every act were written down the whole world would not have enough room for the books that would have to be written. Only the most grudging, the hardest of unbelieving hearts, could reject the basic honesty of the witness to this chapter.

SIX

—

SOME SIGNIFICANT OMISSIONS

The first notable omission is any account of Jesus's life before his baptism. The writer will have known what Matthew and Luke had worked out but will have realised how inadequately these accounts had been sourced. He knew the scriptures far better than they did. He also knew that any reliable information was no longer available. All he makes clear is that the family was based in Galilee, his father being Joseph, his mother Mary, that Joseph had been a joiner and, by implication, that Jesus had been engaged in this work too.

An important general omission is the actual naming of all the disciples anywhere in the Gospel. We may remember that lists *were* given in the other Gospels but these do not always tally with each other. In John only some core disciples are named, while the description of them as 'The Twelve', to fit the twelve tribes of Israel, may well be traditional. Similarly, the number involved in the feeding of the five thousand may be traditional rather than based on a reliable estimate. There is also an indication that the group may have been somewhat fluid: in John 6:66 a significant number of disciples is said to have given up, although Jesus then addresses the core group, described as the chosen twelve, and we deduce from the account that none of these deserted. Once again, it is Peter who speaks for them all. He is the leader and the witness not only makes this clear but implies, in effect, complete satisfaction with this state of affairs.

Another general omission is an account of any of the parables which we find in the other three Gospels. It would appear that the witness did not tell the writer about them, which suggests that the witness did not have the sort of mind that remembered such things; he remembered events vividly and the conversations tied to the line of development of these events but, like some pupils, he did not have a mind that was attuned to more abstract, more theoretical matter. Parables may not have been to the writer's taste either, although there are plenty of parables in the Gospel which are implicit rather than explicit.

The first important specific omission is the actual fact that there was a baptism. As has been argued before, the writer felt that Jesus was more of the world above than of this world below, more God than man, and so worldly influence, let alone worldly power, should not ever appear to be greater than Jesus. How could God, even in human form, be in need of such intervention, anyway? Similarly, Jesus is never, in this Gospel, said to pray, except as a form of teaching aloud to his disciples. How could one imagine God praying to himself? Nevertheless, the baptism is implied in the information about the breath of God descending upon Jesus, in the form of a dove, and that this was the signal telling John the Baptist that Jesus was to be God's special representative on earth.

The next omission is any mention of the Temptation, which is not at all surprising, as the idea of God being subject to temptation is obviously absurd. Nonetheless, the probability of the temptation having occurred is strong, for why should such an event have been invented by the other Gospel writers? It contributes nothing to the aura of divinity that all the writers wanted to be associated with Jesus. However, John's account of the early days of the ministry leaves no room for it while it would not be in character for the writer to deceive with a contrived misdescription of events. We may assume, therefore, that there probably was a 'temptation', but that it happened before the baptism, which also makes far more sense.

The next omission of interest is the rejection of the chance to accept that John the Baptist, a prophetic voice whose like had not been heard in Israel for centuries, might be Elijah returning to herald the coming of the Messiah and to start the next phase in Jewish history. Mark started his Gospel trying to give this impression. Incidentally, the frequent demotion of John in comparison with Jesus indicates that the writer was trying to reduce the influence of a group which regarded John as more important than Jesus. It could be that the writer's deep knowledge of scripture had alerted him to the idea that John the Baptist was the one referred to, when Isaiah wrote chapter 40:3, as the voice of one crying in the wilderness, "Prepare the way of the Lord." At one stroke he had 'demoted' the Baptist and elevated Jesus by making John merely his herald.

A surprising omission is the Transfiguration, at which John the witness was said to have been present. The strong probability of this occurring in some form is Peter's saying to Jesus (Mark 9:5) 'We should erect three tents: for you, one, one for Moses and one for Elijah.' The sign of truth is the added comment about Peter, 'for he did not know what to say.' If these details were artifice, they are beyond the narrator skills of the author of Mark and would have to have been added in much more modern times. Not only do they validate the story, but indicate that only Peter would have supplied such information, thus confirming that the source of information for Mark's Gospel is Peter himself. It would seem quite extraordinary for the witness not to have remembered such an occasion and not to have told the writer about it. It would seem unlikely that the writer would not have mentioned it, had he been told about it, even if it does appear in the first three Gospels, from which the writer is distancing himself; after all, he gives an account of the feeding of the five thousand. It is just possible that the witness failed to provide this information, or that it was included in an original account from the writer but has since been lost or, also possible, that Peter was in a trance when he witnessed it, and John was not. They were up a mountain: might the climb have affected Peter? Or was the information that the brothers, James and John, were there when it happened, wrong?

A most notable omission from John's account of the Last Supper is the giving of the bread with 'This is my body' and, at the end of the supper, the wine with 'This is my blood,' followed by the instruction that we should continue to do this in memory of Jesus. It seems even stranger, when we consider the trouble Jesus caused by saying, in some form, that people had to eat his flesh and drink his blood if they were to gain spiritual salvation. It may be that the young witness disciple was out of the room or asleep when it happened or that, for some reason not yet provided, the writer decided that this particular event did not need to be recorded after what he had said before, or was not sufficiently important theologically. Of course, it might have been in the original version, but that particular part of it lost. Or, again, could it be that it was somehow missed out by an oversight?

Another omission is the long period, supposedly in the garden, of prayers made by Jesus before he was arrested, which John places during the time *before* he went to the garden, and more like public supplications to God, rather than normal prayers. Once again, Jesus would not be praying to God if he *were* God, rather than God's special agent. An even more significant omission, which appears in Mark (15:34) and is repeated by Matthew (27:46), is the passage taken from Psalm 22:1, translated as 'My God, my God, why hast thou forsaken me?' which Jesus uttered on the cross. The fact that a misunderstanding is reported – 'Is he calling on Elijah?' – suggests that this was actually said. It is a very significant omission, so long as it was actually uttered and reported to the writer by the witness; it emphasises that Jesus is not God, else how can God forsake God? Incidentally, 16:28, we have Jesus leaving the world and going to the Father: he would not be going to himself so Jesus, yet again, is portrayed as *not* being God. It is also significant, as John attributed to Jesus a claim that God was with him (16:32). Did God really leave Jesus and was it so that his death on the cross should be hastened? If he were alive on the cross for only six hours, as recorded elsewhere (Mark 16:25-38), his speedy death might lend support to this theory. The streams of blood and plasma from his pierced side suggest that Jesus might indeed have died of grief. William Barclay offers this argument in his commentary on this Gospel.

Another omission is the tradition that Simon of Cyrene carried the transverse beam of the cross for Jesus. It might be that the witness was unable to follow closely enough during this part of the journey because of the pressure of the crowds or, perhaps, he was so overwhelmed with grief that he did not notice anything at this particular stage.

There will be other signifiant omissions.

–

EPILOGUE

The first point to be made is that we have in the last Gospel stories that cannot rationally be rated as fiction. We have preserved in these what may be the almost unvarnished truth. A careful examination of the evidence proves that Jesus understood and loved his fellows; he taught and healed. It also proves, almost as certainly, that he reappeared, in a disembodied, often unrecognised form, to those who had been his closest followers. The last piece of evidence is that we still have the religion that stemmed from his ministry: it endures to this day.

This booklet has been written with the intention of finding the truth and correcting possible misconceptions. This is another correction:

> How good of God to choose the Jews;
> And twice as good: the Jews chose God.

This is far nearer the truth than the old version which we knew as:

> How odd of God to choose the Jews;
> But not so odd, the Jews chose God.

It is true that some Greek philosophers had calculated that there should be some unchanging, immanent but indescribable and, in effect, eternal and infinite being that was not anthropomorphic; it may be true that Socrates was said to have had special experiences when he had powerful sensations that he should not do what he had in mind; however, these people did not choose to single out this being for special reverence and devotion. The Jews, on the other hand, did. They were the people who chose to worship the one and only God, the tradition starting, effectively, with Abraham as the first real Jew, even if the rather unattractive Jacob was the first to have the name Israel. It was Isaiah who explained that the Jewish faith was for all peoples on earth; it is Jesus the Jew who has made this possible.

There is a corollary: according to what we read in Matthew, and this is in accord with what we may understand from reading John's Gospel, Jesus, as well as showing the true way to God, also said in Matthew

7:15-18, "Beware of false prophets, who come to you in sheep's clothing [e.g. beguiling language] but inwardly are ravening wolves [seeking benefit for themselves or their own families, or their own areas or ethnic peoples]. You will know them by their fruits [e.g. profiteering, vengeful murders, destruction, vandalism, terrorising talk]. Are grapes gathered from thorns, or figs from thistles? So every sound tree bears good fruit [goodwill that improves the lives of others], but the bad tree bears evil fruit [arrogant, selfish, intolerant, malevolent, sadistic behaviour]. A sound tree cannot bear evil fruit, nor can a bad tree bear good fruit. Every tree that does not bear good fruit is cut down and thrown into the fire. Thus *you will know them by their fruits.*" We have also, in Matthew 12:34, 2nd half and v. 35, "For out of the abundance of the heart the mouth speaks. The good man out of his good treasure brings forth good, and the evil man out of his evil treasure brings forth evil."

We need to recognise the truth but we may also need to know what we should steer clear of. This booklet is intended to help us do this.

–

AFTERTHOUGHT

John Ashton, in his 'Understanding the Fourth Gospel', struggles with the truth, as it is hidden behind the screen of his tradition-bound thinking and reading. For him the stories of the resurrection are mesmerising fancy, akin to beliefs in Santa Claus; children wake, as they learn more about the real world, from these comforting dreams so that their former exciting belief changes into humdrum unbelief. Ashton, although he does not mention the views and arguments of Richard Dawkins, may have been infected with the scepticism which these express. With a relatively closed mind he has missed the evidence that suggests that the writer of the Fourth Gospel had his unbelief converted into belief. The powerful mind of that writer, filled with the teaching of obviously convinced evangelists, may have been struggling vainly to account for these stories of resurrection and other miracles. Suddenly, he encounters the ageing witness to 'acts of Jesus'. What had been almost unbelievable fairy stories are suddenly shown somehow to be real after all. This is a major driving force in the mind of the writer of the Fourth Gospel, even though he did not appreciate how the 'miracles' and the resurrection were actually explicable in terms that may accord with the experiences that may be met in our everyday world. Matter once dismissed as having nothing more than fairy tale substance suddenly seems to him to have donned the clothes of reality, of divine truth. He may not be able to explain what he has just learned, but this new learning has now overwhelmed him so that he can no longer completely disbelieve. He explains the paradox of apparently unearthly and otherwise impossible feats by endowing Jesus with unearthly, thus heavenly, powers. He has made Jesus into God. Neither the writer then, nor Ashton so much more recently, has understood matters as the witness's statements actually indicated, provided one has read 'between the lines'. All the miracles almost certainly happened but they are not miracles, just instances of the truth being so much stranger than everyday fiction. Believing in a factual basis for the truth of the 'Christian' message is just as easy for a rigorous scientist as it is for anyone else. None of us should ever feel defeated.

John Ashton, *Understanding the Fourth Gospel, 2nd. edition*, OUP. 2007, p. 486: "Neither the resurrection itself nor the stories told to illustrate its significance are historical in any meaningful sense of the word. Anyone who disagrees with this statement has a lot of puzzles to wrestle with, puzzles for which, I am convinced, no solutions are available." Could it be that this wonderful scholar is being as blind, in this particular belief, as others, such as Richard Dawkins?

—

RUMINATION AFTER LOOKING AT KEITH WARD'S 'THE TURN OF THE TIDE'

HOW MIGHT THE TIDE ACTUALLY BE TURNED?

Canon Ward is Emeritus Professor of the History and Philosophy of Religion at King's College, London, so it could be noted that some philosophy has been primarily concerned with language, which is secondary, as opposed to the primary ideas to which language and its usage give shape. Some Philosophers have tried to operate with language as if words are the equivalent of mathematical symbols, which, themselves, are primary, in that they present ideas in forms which may be examined and manipulated independently of anything else; language, being secondary, cannot be safely used as if it is primary. Conclusions reached, operating with language which is being used normally, without sufficient reference to the underlying ideas, are not guaranteed to be completely accurate or even useful. We may have read that Wittgenstein pronounced that '**Meaning** [meaning does not normally become 'visible', intelligible, transmissible until it is shaped in *language*, whether verbally or bodily] **is use**.' Did he know what he really meant? Did these particular words satisfactorily clothe his thoughts so that one would fully comprehend the ideas to which these words were intended to give shape? One should remember that, just as spelling is an attempt to give form to sounds, words are supposed to show the intended shape of ideas, of thoughts. Most people do not or, rather, cannot show by their choice of spelling, however cunningly contrived, with commiserations to Robert Burns, exactly how they themselves pronounce words; in a comparable situation, words try to give shape to ideas, but necessarily fail, on almost every occasion, to show the precise shape of the ideas which they are supposed to be clothing. Without words or models, ideas are incommunicable, probably even to ourselves, but the words, however well-chosen, cannot usually be perfect for their tasks and will fail in their intended purposes to greater or lesser extents. Further, when one person uses a word, the understanding of the precise meaning of that word on the part of the hearer, seer (sign language) or reader may be different from that of the user; the contexts, in which different people acquire the understanding of words, are necessarily different, one from another, so, as words have meaning according to their past and present contexts, every user of a word has an understanding of that word which is different from that of every other user. Words 'live' and develop in the foreground of ever receding contextual landscapes of meaning, suiting those receding landscapes in the manner of chameleons set in a continuously changing background. Language restricts and may even distort the ideas to which it is supposed to give intelligible form. One might remember, in this exposition, the horror story (Ambrose Bierce?) in which the malignant ghostly power is invisible until it dons a sheet to give itself a terrifying, twisting, visible shape. Ideas are 'invisible', incommunicable until words or models give them 'perceptible' form.

Therefore, as has been said, philosophers are in error if they think that language is primary in the sense that Mathematics may be thought to be, and that language may be worked on in the same way as mathematical ideas may be, as if words are mathematical symbols in quasi-mathematical equations, unless this is achieved in Formal Logic, for which an examination paper might ask, "Is this a question?", to which an ordinary language user might answer, "Yes, if this is an answer", and fail to have answered satisfactorily: the fact that the antecedent for the demonstrative pronoun 'this' is unstated has not been pointed out. Language is secondary, not primary, so constructing things in words, and then manipulating and examining those words so as to draw conclusions, without adequate reference to the ideas to which the words are meant to give 'visible' shape, must be logically mistaken.

Unhappily, there are further problems in that words distort the shapes of people's ideas while they are clothing them in words, and the words themselves not only take their meanings from their contexts, but also, like rivers, into which one cannot step into the same one twice, are endlessly, though usually very gradually, changing their meanings and influence during the process of people using them. Occasionally, it is true, a word's change of meaning may be rapid: 'candour' used to mean the euphemistically 'whitewashing' of someone or something, but Sheridan's 'School for Scandal' character, Mrs. Candour, changed the usage of that word so that 'candour' very soon came to signify the opposite. Similarly, spelling may have been misconceived for its purpose and so results in changes of pronunciation which not everyone finds very satisfactory.

There is the demanding corollary, that those who have ideas need a lexical command which meets their own needs and is right for those of the hearers, seers or readers. Making matters worse, lexical command is not carefully attended to these days, so that words such as 'epicentre' are used where they do not really apply, just because the user thinks they sound more impressive than the correct but simpler items, while some words, such as 'contagious' and 'infectious', are used as if their meanings are the same. Ignorance may be bliss for some, but the display of that ignorance, particularly on the part of personnel in the Media, may be very irritating for others and even result, possibly, in damaging misunderstanding. Unfortunately, the Media, although the BBC, for instance, is to be congratulated for its collaboration with Professor Ward for the 1986 Radio 4 series that gave rise to this book and for many other similar ventures, seem rather too often, to be more concerned with attracting audiences with bread-and-circuses trivia than dealing with, albeit less interesting, matters of more moment and greater educational importance.

Wittengenstein provides important examples of what should concern us. Sir Anthony Kenny, in his book, 'A Brief History of Western Philosophy', remarks that Wittengenstein lost his faith at school, while Professor Ward claims that Wittengenstein insisted on describing himself as a Roman Catholic throughout his life. Kenny 'lost' his faith while he was practising as a priest while Ward 'found' his faith when still young. Two different pictures, although they do not actually conflict, from two different mind-sets. However, it is the character of Wittengenstein's philosophical thinking that illustrates the problem; he was concerned with thoughts, meaning and its clarification, language and the various ways in which words work, knowledge, with specific reference to defining propositions, and the possibilities of verification and falsification. Yet he, one of the most influential philosophers of the first half of the twentieth century, seemed to think that faith was to be considered separately from material reality. Mind, also, is sometimes thought of as something abstract, and so, somehow, not totally connected with or dependent on our material world. Verification or falsification of the bases of faith seemed to him a matter that need not be addressed. Faith was disconnected from reason; whether the Gospels were true or false was not a matter that seemed suitable for philosophical investigation. He appeared to be unaware, in his apparent dismissal of 'reason' as underlying what the Gospels had to say, that there might be some statements that were supported by evidence and others that were not. Sir Anthony Kenny, we know, is aware of the importance of whether God exists or not, but Wittengenstein seemed not to be. Yet, it should be absolutely clear to everyone that if God exists, this is a matter of fundamental importance and it should determine the shape of our lives: religion is not a totally separate activity from the rest of what we think, feel, say and do. Judaism, as an example, is about how one should conceive and conduct the whole of one's life, not just one segment of it, so to declare, for instance, that rabbis should refrain from making political statements, is manifestly absurd.

It is possible that particular claims made by some 'Christians' have caused problems. Jesus, for them, is the closest we may come to God, and so the closest to being infallible, yet even Jesus is described as implying that he is not God and also as saying that God knew some things which he did not. If this principle is accepted, no human should make claims for which there is no evidence, even though there may be belief, on the part of the claimant, that the claims *ought* to be true. No human is, or ever was, infallible. We might think of the nineteenth century dogmatically defined decision that the Pope was infallible when he spoke ex cathedra, and the decision irrevocable by any successor. Pope Pius IX decreed in 1854 the doctrine of the Immaculate Conception to be infallible in his bull, Ineffabilis Deus. The First Vatican Council in 1869-70, in its Pastor Aeternus decree, declared that the pope was infallible when he spoke 'ex Cathedra' on matters of faith or morals. Pope Pius XII issued such a declaration in 1950, when he decided that it should be an article of faith that the Virgin Mary had been assumed bodily into heaven, without dying normally - as if heaven were a place in the same way as Rome is a place. To the disgrace of Pope and priest, a lady from North Oxford, who said she could not believe this new and unwarranted assertion, was excommunicated. To suggest that anyone, even a pope, might be infallible in special circumstances, seems indefensible when one remembers the crusades, particularly the Albigensian Crusade which involved the most appalling and totally unchristian treatment of heretical victims and the murder of other innocent people, whose lands the invaders decided to take for themselves of at the 'invitation' of Pope Innocent III. The sale of indulgences was another despicable ruse used to obtain totally unwarranted sums of money for a self-seeking collection of worldly-minded priests. Fallible humans, by definition, are unlikely ever to be infallible. Even when humans feel that it is God who is speaking through them, they cannot be sure of this, nor can anyone else be either. There are many dubious assertions, extant in Christian creeds and scripture, for which no evidence was adduced at the time of their 'publication', some of which assertions were made even before, we may guess, the first Gospels were written. We may want to believe something, but the wish to believe it does not make it true. It was quite correctly perceived that Jesus's message was, as a whole, unique, and thus a unique birth and life were considered only right. However, the evidence was neither provided then nor has such evidence been found since. It is not unreasonable to disbelieve claims that lack supporting evidence; disbelief in claims when they seem impossible in normal human circumstances is even more justifiable. The Gospels are riddled with many such quite improbable claims and these claims may seriously undermine the credibility of the carrier of this vitally important message. An examination of the Gospels, to establish what is likely to have happened, and what is less likely, is now urgently needed to make the truth more accessible for those who cannot bring themselves to believe what is apparent nonsense.

Another area of interest may be the ontological argument about whether the existence of God can be proved. This would appear to be fairly readily addressed. We live in a material world, material in that our senses perceive it, which is subject to creation, change, decay and destruction, while our idea of God is of an eternal unchanging entity who exists in a totally different manner from us and in a way that is beyond and outside our experience. It does not make obvious sense, for instance, to claim that we have been made in the image of God, when it is impossible for us to know anything at all about God, except to calculate that we are his creation, his children. Therefore, as it is impossible for us to perceive God directly, it is impossible for us to prove directly that God exists. We may infer God's existence, but we cannot properly prove that God exists employing solely material criteria. A further point to be borne in mind is that we, as humans, may attribute defined purposes to the actions of other humans, but we cannot logically, by definition, try to calculate whether God has purpose or purposes; while trying to define anthropomorphically any such purpose or purposes is even more futile. This is not a matter of revering God as we should but of whether we can conceivably understand what, by definition, is, for us, incomprehensible. We are often not very good at understanding one another, so to imagine that any of us can understand God at all, in any way, is foolishness beyond measure: we cannot attribute 'purpose' to God, let alone try to calculate what that purpose might be. All we can do is hope that guidance from God may come into our minds, be fully and correctly perceived, and then successfully followed, although precisely how such guidance may come to be imparted we cannot know; as Professor Ward makes clear, this is not necessarily an easy process.

Before making more comments, it is worth pointing out that there are a great many different religious faiths at the moment, some of which conflict with one another as to what they claim to be true. If there is only one God, although each of us will have different paths to travel from our different positions towards our divine destinations, the truth is probably rather more circumscribed than the wild variety of faiths and their constituent components might otherwise suggest. It would seem that insufficient attention has been paid to looking for and examining carefully all the factual evidence which is believed to support the claims made. Unsurprisingly, some faiths imply, or even state, that basic claims made by other faiths, which are seen as competitors, are false. If such statements are made by a faith, these claims should be examined particularly carefully, as an analysis of them might provide revelatory conclusions about the character and base of the faiths concerned; some allegations may be shown to be tantamount to fraud, defamatory and false, thus, in effect,'convicting' the claimant and so undermining that claimant's trustworthiness while, at the same time, strengthening the claims of the faith under attack. Searching out, and then examining, evidence for truth in religious beliefs, seems not to have been done often enough. This is partly because religious beliefs are so important to many people, that undermining their beliefs is considered harmful both to them and to others. However, just as being able to rely on the ground beneath our feet, on which we confidently step, being strong enough to support us matters, so it also matters that the religious beliefs, on which we rely, by which we are guided, be sufficiently strongly based in truth. We establish the reliability of that truth by looking for and then examining the evidence. It may be suggested that insufficient work has been done in this respect as regards religious beliefs. We need, also, to examine the internal evidence in creeds and scriptures. If a creed and its scriptures claim to be for the world, there should not be in that creed or those scriptures any fundamental claims or obligations that might seem to restrict that creed or those scriptures to only one era, or to only one language, or one race, or place, or culture. A worldwide religion will be timeless, its ideas and teaching equally intelligible and appreciable in any language. It will be for every race, for every sort of person, whether clever or not, whether educated or not, whether suffering from mental or physical disabilities or not. What we believe affects what we do and what we do matters to the world. It is much more than just important that we get our beliefs right; it is vital.

An early question in Keith Ward's Preface is 'Has Christian morality collapsed?'. There are so many different influences affecting the current situation that an appropriate answer could be, 'Yes, at least to some extent'. The teaching of Christianity in schools is dangerously reduced; aggressive behaviour in society is far more prevalent, partly because schooling is now so absorbed with the acquisition of the knowledge of facts, without learning how to think dispassionately so as to be able to use that knowledge profitably, that a proper understanding of interpersonal responsibility and an awareness of proportional importance are not grasped by most of the population; Edward de Bono tried to help us address the importance of learning how to think effectively, but the politicians and education experts seem to have found this too inconvenient to bother with. Thus we have a society that does not see clearly what needs attention, because it operates in a dense fog of facts, whose possible utility is very often not fully appreciated; the use of language is becoming habitually careless - whether it be lexical precision, consistent pronunciation or correct usage of grammar and syntax - and so, as most of us think with words, our thought processes are sloppier and less precise too; the social network is now so complicated that human mental capacity, which was adequate for our needs two millennia earlier, is no longer adequate for current demands, and this effect is increased by the exponential rate of expansion in the development of IT resources; the effect of bypassing many population-control 'mechanisms' in our species has resulted in serious overpopulation which promotes aggressive behaviour; the importance of money has eclipsed the importance of almost everything else, as we hear when we are told that the value of a university education is primarily to be assessed by its monetary value later in life. Money, which is amoral because it is inanimate, is now more highly valued than morality.

Not long after I was born in 1934, Alfred Ayer asserted, in his book, 'Language, Truth and Logic',1936, that the word God was without meaning, because the actual existence of God was, he also decided, unverifiable. He was immediately believed by a large and influential group of gullible people. This was a curious claim to make, as the existence of some forms of matter is 'verified' by observing how observable matter is affected in ways that are thought to be explicable only if not yet observed and possibly unobservable forms of matter actually exist and and, in some way, produce the observed effects. How is it possible to deny that there might possibly be observable effects in our universe that are explicable only by the existence of an unobservable god? It is true that later on Ayer is said to have admitted that the existence of God might be posited as an explanatory hypothesis, but he then went on to declare that he would still dismiss the proposition that God existed on the grounds that this explained nothing: what arrogance to claim such omniscience! The fact that he himself has not found anything that lacked an explanation that the existence of God would otherwise provide does not mean that there is nothing to be found by someone else. Just as blindly arrogant is Ayer's assertion that he is right to say, 'One reason for not believing Christianity is that there is not the slightest evidence in its favour. So I do not believe it any more than I believe there is a rhinoceros the room.' The moment someone produces an irrelevant and ridiculous rhinoceros point to support an argument, one senses that there may be weakness in that argument. One is reminded of some of the arguments advanced in his book, 'The God Delusion', by Professor Dawkins. Being too lazy to look for and then analyse evidence dispassionately does not prove that the lazy arguer is right.

However, to declare that experiencing something in

some way is unnecessary to arrive at a belief, would seem wrong, as all our beliefs and thought processes derive, ultimately, from our neurological reactions and actions, which have their stimulus origins in sensory experience, including mental events and the processes following those events, however much thinking may influence the course of assessing the meaning of those experiences. God has given us a real material world to understand with our senses and then to manage as well as we are able; we demonstrate our love for God by doing just that.

Nevertheless, when someone declares that belief in God is the same sort of fundamental belief as the belief that objects continue to exist when we are not observing them, there is glaring illogicality: we can see and, possibly, experience objects directly in many ways, but we can experience God only indirectly, even when we sense, somehow, that it is God who is intervening directly in what we are experiencing at a particular moment.

As an aside, it might be noted that the assertion that the only things that exist are material objects in space, is as illogical as the atheism of which it is an extension; it would seem to be another form of logical positivism, which seems to have been discredited very many years ago. Possibilities are theoretically infinite, so proving the negative, which the claim to the non-existence of what is not perceived implies, is not logically possible.

There are, it should be admitted, two apparently insoluble central difficulties when it comes to claiming that God created the world and all the attendant universe. Why did God do so? And if immaterial souls drive our material bodies so that there is somehow freewill, how does this happen? Incidentally, if the soul is to the body as a driver is to a car, how can we know that a body is being driven by same soul throughout that body's existence? Taking the second, though less important, point first, how does something that is immaterial affect something that is material, since there is not a demonstrably logical relation with what it affects? This is crucial, because if there is no freewill, the existence of which would seem explicable only if something immaterial can intervene, God becomes the God of the deists. How does one electron have a mind and powers of its own and then decide to act in a way that changes the course of any sequence of behaviour? Belief in freewill is cardinal. Even more difficult is the first point: why did God create us all in the first place? All we can do, I fear, is follow Alexander Pope when he writes, "Presume not God to scan." God's purpose in creating us may well be unknowable, but the fact that it may be unknowable does not vitiate Theism. We may feel we know that God exists and that what we do matters to God, but we are not in a position, as we do not have the appropriate mental and sensory resources, to speculate profitably about God and his purposes. It is argued here that finding evidence for the existence of God, and further evidence of what God wants from us, is what matters: if we can manage, somehow, to do just that, that is all that is necessary.

It may be feared that statements, such as 'Religion is about worship and prayer', are dangerously elliptical, as it is behaviour that demonstrates, for the most part, what is driving that behaviour. Remembering James saying in his New Testament letter that faith without works is vain, we demonstrate worship in how we treat the world and all that is in it, following the words of George Herbert in his hymn, "And what we do in anything to do it as for thee." The prayer we make will be that we may be enabled to do that. Worship without works is not very different from faith without works, while prayer should be for something that makes us perform better for God and in God's eyes. One might add that going to Church, if one goes to Church as a form of escape from the uncomfortable challenges with which the world confronts us, is little different from going to the cinema: a possibly pleasurable experience, and respite, but not necessarily one that will show us how to lead better lives in the real world so as to make life better for everyone else, and thereby for ourselves. We should note here that Christianity is supposed to be about how one should direct one's whole life, so pretending that this does not involve thinking politically is arrant nonsense.

If we review Christianity, or New Judaism, which might be a more accurate description, we might remember the 'Lord's Prayer' whose first sentence declares that God is our Father and goes on to pray "Hallowed be thy name" (which implies that we should never use the name 'God' without feeling active respect for that name) and continues with the words, "Thy kingdom come; thy will be done in earth as it is in heaven." The kingdom is one of universal goodwill in which our practised form of life is one in which self-interest, envy, hatred and pride are set aside so that we build up a worldwide community of mutual service and responsibility. Mankind has been given responsibility for managing this world, so we are responsible for most of what goes wrong. We cannot rationally blame God. Instead we should pray to God to help us see how we may put some things right and make other things better, so that the world becomes more like the world which God would like us to build.

When we view the world in which we live, we see much that is wrong, which an accurate picture of our responsibilities - and how these *are* our responsibilities - would help us to want to put right. To arrive at a convincing explanation of what our duties are and why, we should try to think more carefully about the evidence and where that leads. If we consider beliefs that are thought by many to be central to Christianity, we might think of the concept of a virgin birth and miracles in which the dead are brought back to life even when the body is thought to have decayed sufficiently for it to stink. It is, in effect, believed by some 'Christians' that God needs miracles as proof that he exists, and that without these beliefs in the miraculous our faith is greatly weakened, if not demolished. God does not need miracles to prove anything to us, so we should not need miracles to confirm our faith. The early Jews, such as the first Jew, Abraham, did not need miracles at the beginning to come to believe in the one and only God, even though the Old Testament recounts stories in which God shows that there is a living God, when the other 'opposing' gods, by contrast, are shown to have no powers, no proof of existence, why should we need special proof when the early Jews did not? Careful and dispassionate examination of the evidence can reveal a different set of explanations for the truth in Jesus's teaching that is just as convincing as any so-called Christian might wish to discover. Indeed, it may be suggested that some 'Christian' beliefs, considered at present to be both essential and fundamental, might be described as destructive rogue white elephants, disguised as peaceable sacred cows, rampaging in the shop displaying the tenets of 'Christianity' . This is important, as when there is conflicting testimony, the proper way to decide which claims are right is not to say more people say this rather than that, so this has to be the right answer; nor this case has been believed by millions for many centuries, so it would not be false; similarly, having more extravagant claims than the other side does not prove that this is superior to that; again being more threatening than one's opponents - you will be condemned to eternal punishment if you do not do as we tell you, as everyone else is wrong and only we are right - does not prove one's opponents to be wrong; saying that the new claims are right because, in effect, they are more recent and more dogmatic than the old claims and superior to anything that has appeared before, is not valid; the fact that one set of claims may come in the most beguiling language that might be imagined is no proof of authenticity either. When there is a dispute about which set of claims is more likely to be right, it is the available evidence and the analysis of that evidence which should decide which is the more likely truth. What is false may be dressed in the most alluring and, indeed, wonderfully mesmerising clothes, but, despite compelling appearances and hypnotising sounds, it is still false. It is sound, honest evidence that is needed to be unearthed and examined so as to arrive at what is true.

The internal evidence may be extremely important, but any external evidence, if such can be found, is important too. Therefore, one should note the tradition in the Babylonian Talmud, a completely non-'Christian' source, which relates that one Yeshu (Jesus) was hung (crucified) on the eve of the Passover, for sorcery and leading Israel astray. This is hugely important evidence that Jesus existed, healed, exorcised, taught and was crucified on the eve of the Passover. The evidence of what Jesus did and taught exists, but too many additional extras have been appended, and these extras are often seen as more compelling and important than the original much more probable facts. As a result, these additions obscure reality. When truth is hidden beneath a plethora of superfluous, unwarranted material, this camouflage may deceive many, although not necessarily for the long term; however, those who seek clear truth will be less delighted and are less likely to be deceived by the superficial extras and may even be so put off that further pursuit of underlying truth is abandoned. Evidence for the teaching and death of Jesus and, even more important, evidence for some sort of reappearance after Jesus's death, are cardinal: the evidence is extremely strong. This evidence is stronger than any arguments that may be advanced to contradict its conclusions. Interestingly, as Jesus was a Jew and never renounced his Judaic beliefs, this evidence supports the thesis that Judaism is truly based, even though Jesus taught that great modifications and simplification to the existing Judaic structure, were required by God; Jesus was teaching a new form of Judaism, not a new religion.

As an extra consideration, it should not be imagined that a loving father God would make matters challenging for would-be servants of God with the deliberate intent that some should fail. This is no more credible than the idea that God would intentionally lead unbelievers astray so that they might then be consigned to eternal fires fuelled by men and stones. Only small children build to then destroy with hoots of laughter.

This book, *Where is the Evidence? Finding the Truth in the Gospel of John*, aims to find firsthand evidence and explain how we may safely trust its reliability. It should be acknowledged that some of the conclusions in the book, which is a summarising paraphrase of an earlier book, 'A New Vision', will be rejected outright because, although good evidence supports the claims, contrary traditional beliefs are even more strongly held than were those traditional beliefs that resulted in the rejection of the claims of Galileo, when he pointed out that the earth went round the sun and not the sun round the earth. However, truth should be admitted and allowed to prevail. We shall then have a truly stronger chance of making the world, in which we all live inescapably together, a better place.

This book is printed on paper from sustainable sources managed under the Forest Stewardship Council (FSC) scheme.

It has been printed in the UK to reduce transportation miles and their impact upon the environment.

For every new title that Matador publishes, we plant a tree to offset CO_2, partnering with the More Trees scheme.

For more about how Matador offsets its environmental impact, see www.troubador.co.uk/about/